GREAT AUTHORS OF

# POPULAR
# FICTION

Essential Authors
for Children & Teens

GREAT AUTHORS OF

# POPULAR
# FICTION

EDITED BY HOPE KILLCOYNE

**Britannica**®
Educational Publishing
IN ASSOCIATION WITH

**ROSEN**
EDUCATIONAL SERVICES

Published in 2014 by Britannica Educational Publishing (a trademark of Encyclopædia Britannica, Inc.) in association with The Rosen Publishing Group, Inc.
29 East 21st Street, New York, NY 10010

Distributed exclusively by Rosen Publishing.
To see additional Britannica Educational Publishing titles, go to rosenpublishing.com

First Edition

Britannica Educational Publishing
J.E. Luebering: Director, Core Reference Group
Anthony L. Green: Editor, Compton's by Britannica

Rosen Publishing
Hope Lourie Killcoyne: Executive Editor
Nelson Sá: Art Director
Cindy Reiman: Photography Manager
Introduction and supplementary material by Joseph Kampff.

### Cataloging-in-Publication Data

Great authors of popular fiction/editor, Hope Killcoyne.—First edition.
        pages cm.—(Essential Authors for Children & Teens)
Includes bibliographical references and index.
ISBN 978-1-62275-086-3 (library binding)
1. Novelists—Biography—Juvenile literature. I. Killcoyne, Hope L., editor of compilation.
PN452.G698 2014
809—dc23
[B]
                                                                2013027181

*Manufactured in the United States of America.*

# Contents

13

53

64

91

137

159

169

183

# Introduction

With so many authors and books in the world, it is sometimes difficult to know what to read. The number of choices is overwhelming. Often, we look to the popularity of a book or an author for guidance. If so many people are reading it, the logic goes, it must be good. For example, it would have been hard to miss Suzanne Collins's Hunger Games trilogy. All of the books in the series—*The Hunger Games*, *Catching Fire*, and *Mockingjay*—are best sellers. They are extremely popular with teenagers and adults alike. And the Hunger Games trilogy deserves its popularity. The novels are wonderfully imagined and brilliantly plotted, with Collins immersing her readers in a possible future world that is at once fascinating and terrifying.

Even if you have not read the Hunger Games novels, you have probably heard of them, noticed the artwork on their covers, or seen the movie. You may not know, however, that Collins published another series of books for younger readers, the Underland Chronicles, before writing the Hunger Games. And you may know nothing at all about Collins herself. Yet, authors' lives are often as fascinating as their works. *Great*

*Authors of Popular Fiction* is an excellent source of information on popular writers you may already know a little about, but about whom you would like to know more.

This volume will also introduce you to popular authors who, for one reason or another, have evaded your radar. In addition to immediately recognizable American

*Actress Jennifer Lawrence as Katniss Everdeen in The Hunger Games, by Suzanne Collins. Murray Close/©Lionsgate/Courtesy Everett Collection*

authors such as Suzanne Collins, this volume includes writers from a diverse range of places, introducing readers to the cultures and politics of South Africa (Nadine Gordimer), Sweden (Stieg Larsson), and Chile (Isabel Allende), to name a few. You will also find authors of classic works of children's literature, such as S.E. Hinton and Judy Blume, whose books retain their freshness today.

While most of the authors in this collection write primarily for children and young adults, many of them have tremendous crossover appeal. Mark Zusak's best seller *The Book Thief* was marketed to young adults in the United States and to adults in Australia. Despite the marketing strategies, *The Book Thief* has been hugely successful with both age groups around the world. Others usually write for adults but have sometimes ventured into the world of children's literature. Dave Eggers, for example, made a name for himself with his exuberant memoir—*A Heartbreaking Work of Staggering Genius*—and a number of other nonfiction works before writing *The Wild Things*, a novelization of Maurice Sendak's picture book *Where the Wild Things Are*.

Alan Moore and Art Spiegelman, on the other hand, create works for teenagers and adults in a genre usually associated with children. Moore is best known as the creator of the influential graphic novels *V for Vendetta* and *Watchmen*, and Spiegelman's *Maus* books made comics into a respected art form in the United States.

Whether you're looking for the next great book to read or for more information on your favorite writers, *Great Authors of Popular Fiction* is rich in its scope, accuracy, and its power to excite and surprise.

# SHERMAN ALEXIE

(b. 1966– )

S herman Alexie is an American Indian writer whose poetry, short stories, novels, and films about the lives of American Indians are famous around the world. (Alexie uses the term "Indians" instead of

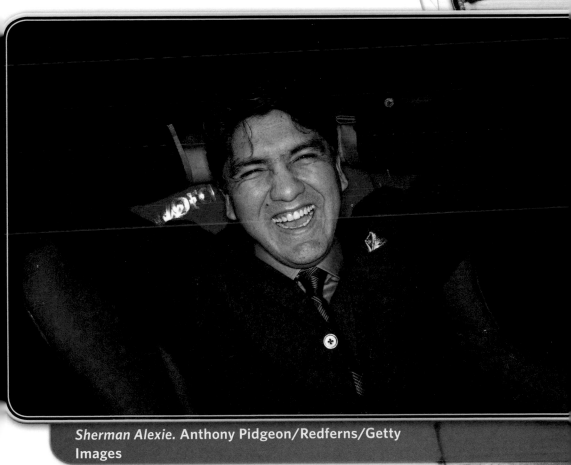

*Sherman Alexie.* Anthony Pidgeon/Redferns/Getty Images

"Native Americans," which he considers an ill-chosen term.) Alexie won the Native Writers' Circle of the Americas Lifetime Achievement Award in 2010.

Born Oct. 7, 1966, on the Spokane Indian Reservation in Wellpinit, Wash., Alexie was immediately diagnosed with hydrocephalus, which literally means "water head." He had surgery when he was a baby to remove the extra fluid from his brain. Because of his poor health, Alexie was unable to participate in many physical activities. Instead, he spent his time reading books and with his grand-mother, a spiritual leader of the Spokane tribe who had an enormous influence on him.

Alexie went to an all-white high school outside of the reservation on which he lived. He was an honour student and class president. His high school experiences pro-vided the basis for *The Absolutely True Diary of a Part-Time Indian* (2007), which won a National Book Award for Young People's Literature. While he was at Washington State University, a poetry course helped him find his voice as a writer.

Alexie is a prolific writer. He published his first volume of poetry, *I Would Steal Horses*, in 1992. The same year, he published

*The Business of Fancydancing*, a book that combined prose and poetry. In 1993, he published two more books of poetry— *First Indian on the Moon* and *Old Shirts & New Skins*—and *The Lone Ranger and Tonto Fistfight in Heaven*, a collection of stories that won the PEN/Hemingway Award for best first book of fiction.

Alexie's first novel, *Reservation Blues* (1995), tells the story of a visit by the blues musician Robert Johnson to Big Mom, a character Alexie based on his own grandmother. The novel examines life on the reservation and the issues facing Indians. His stories in *The Toughest Indian in the World* (2000) won him the PEN/Malamud Award for excellence in short-story writing.

In addition to writing books, Alexie wrote and produced the movie *Smoke Signals* (1998), based on the story "This Is What It Means to Say Phoenix, Arizona" from *The Lone Ranger and Tonto Fistfight in Heaven*. He also wrote and directed the film *The Business of Fancydancing* (2002), which was loosely based on his book of the same name. Alexie is a popular speaker and performer, and has appeared on such television programs as *The Colbert Report*.

# ISABEL ALLENDE

(b. 1942– )

O ne of the first successful woman novelists from Latin America, Isabel
Allende employs magic realism—the use
of fantasy and myth in realistic fiction—to
create stories that reflect her own experiences while they also examine the role of
women in Latin America. Forced to flee
her native Chile for Venezuela after the
1973 assassination of her uncle, Chilean
president Salvador Allende, Allende became
politicized, and her works often include
commentaries on South American politics.
Although thoroughly familiar with the
English language, Allende writes her fiction
in Spanish only. Her work is then translated
into other languages.

Allende was born on Aug. 2, 1942, in
Lima, Peru, to Tomás Allende, a diplomatic
official of Chile, and Francisca Llona. In
1945 Francisca divorced her husband, moving Isabel and her siblings back to Santiago,
Chile, where they moved in with Francisca's
family. When Isabel was nine, her mother
married another diplomat whose appointments would take the family to Bolivia, where

Allende attended a North American–run private school, and Beirut, Leb., where she was enrolled in a British private school.

After finishing her schooling, Allende returned to Santiago. From 1959 to 1965, she worked for the Food and Agriculture Organization of the United Nations, traveling to Europe and living briefly in Switzerland and Belgium with her husband and daughter. In 1966 the family returned to Chile, where she had another child, and in 1967 she began working for the magazine *Paula*, where she was in charge of a humor column. She remained on the staff at the magazine until 1974. During this period she also contributed articles to the children's magazine *Mampato*. Between 1970 and 1975, Allende's career expanded to include forays into writing television shows and a play, *El embajador* (*The Ambassador*), which was produced in 1972.

After her uncle's assassination during the military coup in 1973, Isabel received threats against herself as well as her family, forcing her to flee Chile for Venezuela with her husband and children in 1975. The family settled in Caracas and remained there until 1987, when they moved to the United States. Isabel soon began working for the newspaper *El Nacional*; she also worked for several years as a school administrator.

In 1981 she began writing a letter to her terminally ill grandfather that evolved into her first novel, *La casa de los espíritus* (1982; *The House of the Spirits*). It was followed by the novels *De amor y de sombra* (1984; *Of Love and Shadows*), *Eva Luna* (1987), *El plan infinito* (1991; *The Infinite Plan*), and *Hija de la fortuna* (1999; *Daughter of Fortune*). A collection of stories, *Cuentos de Eva Luna* (*The Stories of Eva Luna*), was published in 1990. The first two novels were eventually made into motion pictures, and *Eva Luna* was adapted as a musical.

Allende's first nonfiction work, *Paula* (1994), was written as a letter to her daughter, who, afflicted with a hereditary blood disease, had fallen into a coma (she died in 1992). After *Paula* was published, Allende suffered from severe writer's block, which she eventually broke through by writing yet another work of nonfiction, *Afrodita: Recetas, cuentos y otros afrodisiacos* (1997; *Aphrodite: Recipes, Stories and other Aphrodisiacs*). *Mi país inventado* (2003; *My Invented Country*) recounted her self-imposed exile after the Sept. 11, 1973, revolution in Chile and her feelings

*Isabel Allende receiving Denmark's top literary award, the Hans Christian Andersen Literature Award, from Denmark's Crown Prince Frederik, Sept. 30, 2012. Claus Fisker/AFP/ Getty Images* about her adopted country, the United States—where she has lived since the early 1990s—after the September 11 attacks of 2001. She published another memoir about her extended family, *La suma de los dias* (*The Sum of Our Days*), in 2007. In 2011 her novel *El Cuaderno de Maya* (*Maya's Notebook*) was published.

In 1990, after democracy was restored in Chile, Allende returned for the first time since her 1975 flight to receive the Gabriela Mistral award. After winning the Chilean National Prize for Literature in 2010, Allende was awarded the Hans Christian Andersen Literature Award in 2012.

# LAURIE HALSE ANDERSON

(b. 1961– )

Laurie Halse Anderson is an American author whose young adult novels take on serious and relevant subjects—such as, rape, post-traumatic stress disorder, and eating disorders—that young adult literature rarely addresses. In addition to her young adult fiction, Anderson has written a number of historical novels for teens and children's picture books.

Anderson was born Oct. 23, 1961, in Potsdam, a town in upstate New York near the Canadian border. She attended Georgetown University, where she earned a bachelor's of science degree in Languages and Linguistics in 1984. Anderson began her writing career working for the *Philadelphia Enquirer*. She published three children's books, *Ndito Runs* (1996), *Turkey Pox* (1996), and *No Time for Mother's Day* (1999), before attaining critical and commercial success with the publication of her first young adult novel, *Speak*, in 1999.

*Speak* relates the story of Melinda, a high school freshman who was raped at a party before the start of the school year. Traumatized by the violence of the rape and the social alienation she suffers afterward—the rapist is an older student she sees regularly at school—Melinda withdraws further and further into herself as the school year progresses. Art class becomes a kind of therapeutic space for Melinda, and she uses art projects to work through her trauma. A *New York Times* best seller and National Book Award finalist, *Speak* became the subject of controversy when a Missouri State University professor, Wesley Scroggins, referred to the novel's depictions of sexual violence as "soft-core pornography," and called for the novel's removal from Missouri high school curriculums. Numerous authors, including Judy Blume, have defended the novel against censorship.

Anderson has since published a number of successful novels for teenagers, including the historical novel *Fever 1793* (2000), *Catalyst* (2002), and 2009's *Wintergirls*, which explores a young woman's struggles with anorexia and the recent death of her childhood best friend. In 2009, Anderson received the Margaret A. Edwards Award from the American Library Association for her significant and enduring contributions to young adult literature.

# WILLIAM H. ARMSTRONG

(b. 1914–d. 1999)

U.S. author and educator William H. Armstrong was best known for his award-winning novel *Sounder*. The novel was a tragic account of a black family's struggle to survive in the rural South at the end of the 19th and beginning of the 20th century.

William Howard Armstrong was born on Sept. 14, 1914, in Lexington, Va. He studied at the Augusta Military Academy from 1928 to 1932 and received a bachelor's degree from Hampden-Sydney College in 1936. He later studied at the University of Virginia and taught history at the Kent School in Connecticut beginning in 1945. Armstrong won a Newbery Medal in 1970 for *Sounder* (1969). The story of a black sharecropper's family and its heroic dog named Sounder was later translated into eight languages and was made into a motion picture in 1972. Armstrong's other works included the novels *The Macleod Place* (1972), *Joanna's Miracle* (1977), and *The Tale of Tawny and Dingo* (1979) and the nonfiction books *The Peoples of the Ancient World* (1959), *Hadassah: Esther, the Orphan Queen* (1972), and *My Animals* (1973). The author also wrote *Study Tips: How to Improve Your Grades* (1981). Armstrong died on April 11, 1999, in Kent, Conn.

# MARGARET ATWOOD

(b. 1939– )

**M**argaret Atwood is a Canadian author whose many imaginative novels, such as *The Handmaid's Tale* (1985) and *Surfacing* (1972), often deal with feminist and gender-related issues. She is also well known for her nonfiction works, poetry and short story collections, children's books, and contributions to the literature and theory of speculative fiction. In addition to writing, Atwood taught English literature at several Canadian and American universities.

Atwood was born in Ottawa, Can. on Nov. 18, 1939. Although her family lived in Toronto, Atwood spent much of her early childhood in the forests of northern Canada where her father did research on insects. She began writing when she was five years old, and her writing became more serious while she was a teenager. After earning a master's degree in English literature from Radcliffe College, Cambridge, Mass., in 1962, Atwood won a scholarship to Harvard University to pursue a Ph.D. degree. Atwood did not finish her dissertation, however, choosing to set aside her research to write novels and screenplays instead.

In her early poetry collections, *Double Persephone* (1961), *The Circle Game* (1964, revised in 1966), and *The Animals in That Country* (1968), Atwood meditates on human behavior, the natural world, and the problems of materialism. Many of Atwood's works focus on women trying to understand their relationship to the world and the people around them. *The Handmaid's Tale* (1985; film 1990) is about a woman living in sexual slavery in a repressive Christian society of the future after a major ecological catastrophe. The Booker Prize–winning *The Blind Assassin* (2000) is a complex novel about an elderly Canadian woman writing a memoir to clear up any confusion about her sister's suicide and her own role in the later publication of a novel supposedly written by her sister. And *Surfacing* (1972) explores the relationship between nature and culture through the story of a woman's return to her childhood home in the northern wilderness of Quebec.

In her 2006 dystopian novel *Oryx and Crake*, Atwood describes a plague-induced apocalypse in the near future through the memories of a protagonist who may be the only human survivor. Atwood returned to the world of *Oryx and Crake* in 2009 with the publication of *The Year of the Flood*, which extended and retold the story from other perspectives.

Atwood also wrote many short stories, which are collected in volumes such as *Dancing Girls* (1977), *Bluebeard's Egg* (1983), *Wilderness Tips* (1991), and *Moral Disorder* (2006). Her nonfiction works include *Negotiating with the Dead: A Writer on Writing* (2002) and *Payback* (2008), a long essay that looks at personal and social debt from a cultural perspective. In her 2011 work *In Other Worlds: SF and the Human Imagination*, Atwood discusses her life as a lover of science fiction while considering many of the major themes with which science fiction deals. She also describes the differences between science fiction and the speculative fiction that she writes.

# LYNNE REID BANKS

(b. 1929– )

Lynne Reid Banks is an English novelist and playwright. Although she is best known for her series of "Indian" children's books, including *The Indian in the Cupboard* (1980), she has written many books on a wide variety of subjects.

Banks was born in London, Eng., July 31, 1929. During World War II, Banks left England with her mother for Saskatoon, Can., where they lived from 1940 until the end of the war in 1945. Her father stayed behind in London to work. Banks returned to London after the war and attended three drama schools, including the prestigious Royal Academy of Dramatic Art. Banks graduated in 1949 and began acting in small theatrical productions around London. Unable to achieve the level of success she desired, Banks gave up acting after five years to become a playwright. The British Broadcasting Company produced her first play, *It Never Rains Twice*, in 1954. Banks has since written numerous works for stage, radio, and television.

Banks's first adult novel, *The L-Shaped Room*, appeared in 1960. The novel tells the story of Jane Graham, an unmarried woman who moves into a seedy London boarding house after her father kicks her out when he finds out she is pregnant. *The L-Shaped Room* was a critical success, and Banks

revisited the protagonist in two later novels, *The Backward Shadow* (1970) and *Two Is Lonely* (1974).

Banks began publishing children's books with her 1973 novel *One More River*. Her 1977 young adult novel, *Dark Quartet: The Story of the Brontës*, won the American Library Association's Best Books for Young Adults Award. Banks's most popular books, *The Indian in the Cupboard* and its sequel, *The Return of the Indian* (1986), tell the story of Omri, a young boy whose plastic Iroquois Indian, Little Bear, comes to life when Omri locks him inside an old bathroom cupboard. Both novels were commercial and critical successes. *The Indian in the Cupboard* won the *New York Times* Outstanding Book of the Year Award in 1981.

# ANN BEATTIE

(b. 1947– )

Ann Beattie's novels and short stories have been praised for their astute portrayals of upper-middle-class New Englanders dissatisfied with their careers and alienated from society and their loved ones. Frequent inclusions of contemporary culture, especially that of the 1970s and 1980s, and a somewhat detached narrative voice have earned her a reputation as an objective observer of her generation. However, Beattie's affectionate humor rendered a sympathetic portrait of her beleaguered characters, many of whom are shown to be surprisingly resilient.

Ann Beattie was born on Sept. 8, 1947, in Washington, D.C., the only child of Charlotte (Crosby) and James A. Beattie. She was raised in the suburbs of the capital. Educated at the American University in Washington, D.C., Beattie earned a bachelor's degree in 1969. In 1970 she received a master's degree from the University of Connecticut. While working toward her doctorate Beattie was encouraged by J.D. O'Hara, a literature professor at the University of Connecticut, to submit her short stories to various literary magazines. After several of her pieces appeared in small journals, she began submitting stories to the *New Yorker*. After rejecting some 20 of her stories, the *New Yorker* printed Beattie's "A Platonic Relationship" in its

*Ann Beattie.* William F. Campbell/Time & Life Pictures/ Getty Images

April 8, 1974, issue, and published two additional stories of Beattie's later that year. Her first collection of short stories, *Distortions* and her first novel, *Chilly Scenes of Winter*, about a man obsessed with reuniting with an estranged lover, were both published in 1976. The two works established Beattie as a chronicler of the disaffection of a generation of idealistic young people who grew up in the 1960s.

Extolled by critics for their sensitive evocation of mood, Beattie's short stories portray people trapped in deteriorating relationships that leave them numb and despondent. Leading aimless and self-centered lives, her characters are driven to impulsive or eccentric behavior by boredom and disappointment. Little explication of her characters' motives is given in Beattie's minimalist prose. Slang and pop culture references provide a purposefully mundane backdrop for the deeper human drama of loneliness, loss, and recovery played out in Beattie's fiction.

*Secrets and Surprises* (1978), *The Burning House* (1982), *Where You'll Find Me* (1986), and *What Was Mine* (1991) are collections of stories, many of which first appeared in the *New Yorker.* Beattie's second novel, *Falling in Place* (1980), depicts the dissolution of a suburban Connecticut family. Despite a positive ending, the novel suggests that no character is responsible for his destiny and that things just "fall into place." The satiric novel *Love Always* (1985) tells of the relationship between a precocious and troubled 14-year-old soap opera star and her aunt, who writes an advice column for the lovelorn. *Picturing Will*, about a six-year-old boy abandoned by a violent father and raised by his working mother and her lover, followed in 1989. In *Another You* (1995) Marshall Lockard, a college English professor, contemplates an affair with a student, while his wife conducts an affair of her own unbeknownst to him. In *My Life, Starring Dara Falcon* (1997) the manipulative and selfish Dara Falcon becomes a compelling role model to a bored and naive woman. *Park City: New and Selected Stories* was published in 1998. *The Doctor's House* (2002) portrays the impact of a despicable father and an alcoholic mother on their adult children. In the unconventional novel *Mrs. Nixon* (2011), Beattie imagined the life of first lady Pat Nixon and also discussed the art of writing. Her other works include the children's book *Spectacles* (1985), which deals with the supernatural, and *Alex Katz* (1987), a collection of essays in art criticism.

From 1975 to 1977 Beattie taught at the University of Virginia, Charlottesville, where she lived. She then held a teaching position at Harvard University in 1977–78. She returned to the University of Virginia to teach during the fall semesters of 1980 and 1982. She often toured, giving lectures and readings of her work. She received a Guggenheim fellowship in 1977. In 1980 the American Academy and Institute of Arts and Letters awarded Beattie its prize for literature.

# JUDY BLUME

(b. 1938– )

J udy Blume, who spent her childhood in Elizabeth, N.J., is an American author who has always delighted in making up stories. Writing both juvenile and adult fiction, Blume's stories feature people and situations identifiable to her wide-ranging audience. While her frankness, first-person narratives, and ability to portray the concerns of her audience with humour have made her a remarkably popular and award-winning author, her works for younger readers often were banned because of objections to their subject matter and language.

After graduating from high school, Blume (born Judy Sussman Feb. 12, 1938, Elizabeth, N.J.) attended New York University and received a bachelor's degree in education in 1960. In 1959 she married John Blume, with whom she had two children. The couple divorced in the 1970s. While enrolled in a continuing education course on writing for children and teenagers, Blume produced a draft of what became her first published book, *The One in the Middle Is the Green Kangaroo* (1969). At about the same time, she published a version of *Iggie's House* in *Trailblazer* magazine; she rewrote it for publication in book form in 1970.

In 1970 Blume made a huge splash in the world of young adult literature with the publication of *Are You There God? It's Me, Margaret*, a preteen novel told from the perspective of Margaret Simon, an 11-year-old girl whose family has moved to a new town. Margaret, who has a Christian mother and a Jewish father, struggles to understand her developing body and her relationship with religion, speaking directly to God about the uncertainties that come with adolescence—her first period, bra size, boys, and understanding of where she fits in among her new classmates, in her family's religious communities, and with God. Many critics praised Blume's willingness to tackle puberty and other sensitive subject matter in an honest and understandable way. Many young readers wrote letters to tell Blume that they identified with Margaret and her dilemmas. Some adults, however, thought the book inappropriate and wanted it removed from library shelves, citing its frank treatment of menstruation and physical development and claiming that it denigrated religion.

Blume solidified her standing as a leading author of novels for young adults. In *Forever* (1975), a story about unmarried teenagers Katherine and Michael experiencing love and sex for the first time, Blume addressed the topic of sex in a way that spoke to readers of the importance of responsibility—Katherine visits a clinic and is given a prescription for birth control pills—while remaining honest, relatable, and nonjudgmental. The book's treatment of teen sex, birth control, and disobedience to parents made it a prime target of book-banning campaigns.

Blume wrote numerous books for middle-school readers, including *Tales of a Fourth Grade Nothing* (1972), *Otherwise Known as Sheila the Great* (1972), *Blubber* (1974), *Superfudge* (1980), *Fudge-a-Mania* (1990), and *Double Fudge* (2002). Between 2007 and 2009 she continued the story of *The Pain and the Great One* (1984) with a series of four chapter books. Like Blume's books for older audiences, her books for younger readers contained language, situations, and concerns that rang true to the age group, ranging from sibling rivalry to bullying. Blume has also written three novels for adults: *Wifey* (1978), *Smart Women* (1983), and *Summer Sisters* (1998).

Inspired by the James Joyce–centered Bloomsday, celebrated on June 16 of each year in honour of Joyce's 1922 novel *Ulysses* (which takes place on a single day, June 16), in 2007 two writers and Blume fans from Portland, Ore., Joanna Miller and Heather Larimer, decided to create a day to celebrate one of their favorite authors. Named Blumesday, the Judy Blume "holiday" is celebrated on June 17 and has featured dramatic readings from her young adult fiction as well as a video chat with the author herself.

# MEG CABOT

(b. 1967–)

Meg Cabot is an American author who is best known as the author of the young adult series *The Princess Diaries*. She has written many best-selling novels in multiple genres, including supernatural mysteries for teenagers under the pseudonym Jenny Carroll and adult romance novels as Patricia Cabot.

Cabot was born Feb. 1, 1967 in Bloomington, Ind. She attended Indiana University, where her father was a professor, and graduated with a degree in fine arts in 1991. After college, Cabot briefly worked as an illustrator before taking a job as assistant manager of an undergraduate dormitory at New York University. She worked at NYU for ten years before publishing the first book of *The Princess Diaries* series in 2000.

*The Princess Diaries, Volume 1* tells the story of a 14-year-old girl living in New

York's Greenwich Village who finds out that her father is the prince of Genovia, a fictional European country. She has to learn how to be a proper princess while dealing with the challenges of being a typical high school freshman. The novel was an American Library Association Top Ten Pick for Reluctant Readers and Best Book Selection. Walt Disney Pictures released film adaptations of the first two books in the series as *The Princess Diaries* (film 2001) and *The Princess Diaries 2: A Royal Engagement* (film 2004). Cabot has since added many volumes to the popular *Princess Diaries* series.

With over 70 books in print, Cabot is an extremely prolific author. Among her many book series are the young adult mysteries 1-800-Where-R-You (initially published under the name Jenny Carroll, and later reprinted as Vanished under Cabot's own name) and the Mediator series of supernatural novels. Cabot has also written stand-alone novels for adults and young adults, contributed numerous short stories to anthologies, and produced a series of preteen novels titled Allie Finkle's Rules for Girls.

# MICHAEL CHABON

(b. 1963– )

Michael Chabon is an American novelist and essayist known for his elegant language, accomplished use of metaphor, and adventurous experiments with various genres, such as science fiction and the detective story. His narratives often feature references to world mythology and to his own Jewish heritage. Chabon was inducted into the American Academy of Arts and Letters in 2012.

Chabon was born May 24, 1963 in Washington, D.C., and grew up in the planned community of Columbia, Md. Columbia is now the second largest city in Maryland, but the town had only existed for two years when Chabon's family arrived. Chabon spent many hours exploring the growing metropolis when he was young.

After earning a bachelor's degree in English at the University of Pittsburgh in 1984, Chabon entered the creative writing program at the University of California, Irvine, where he received an M.F.A. in 1987. His adviser submitted his master's thesis to a New York publisher without his knowledge,

*Michael Chabon.* Ulf Andersen/Getty Images

and Chabon received a record-high advance payment based on the manuscript. It was published as *The Mysteries of Pittsburgh* in 1988 (film 2008). The novel is a coming-of-age story about a gangster's son during his first summer out of college. Because Chabon narrated the protagonist's homosexual experiences directly, he attracted a large gay following.

His next novel, *Wonder Boys* (1995; film 2000), focuses on a weekend in the life of a creative writing professor as he struggles with his personal and professional failures. Chabon had the idea after he was unable to edit the massive manuscript that he originally wanted to be his second novel. Chabon's third novel, *The Amazing Adventures of Kavalier and Clay* (2000), won the Pulitzer Prize in 2001. The novel contains many mythological references, including the golem of Prague, which appears as a metaphor for rebirth and the process of creating a fictional character. Chabon's *The Yiddish Policemen's Union* (2007), which features many elements of the hard-boiled detective story, won the Hugo Award for best science fiction or fantasy novel in 2008. *Telegraph Avenue* (2012) examines race relations as well as corporate domination in this novel centered around a small record shop that is threatened by a rival chain store.

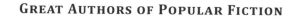

In addition to his novels for adults, Chabon wrote the children's book *The Astonishing Secret of Awesome Man* (2011) and the young adult novel *Summerland* (2002), which features an 11-year-old hero who saves the world from an apocalypse by winning a baseball game against a team of tricksters drawn from American folklore. *Maps and Legends: Reading and Writing Along the Borderlands* (2008) and *Manhood for Amateurs: The Pleasures and Regrets of a Husband, Father, and Son* (2009) are collections of essays that discuss his obsession with various fiction genres and his domestic life. Chabon also wrote a draft of the script for the film *Spider-Man 2* and worked on the screenplay for *John Carter* (2012), a movie adapted from an Edgar Rice Burroughs novel.

# STEPHEN CHBOSKY

(b. 1970– )

S tephen Chbosky is an American screenwriter, film director, and author of the young adult novel *The Perks of Being a Wallflower* (1999).

Chbosky was born Jan. 25, 1970, in Pittsburgh, Pa. He studied screenwriting at the University of Southern California where he earned a bachelor of fine arts degree in 1992. Although he never took a fiction-writing course, Chbosky says that he received the "emotional tools" for writing his novel in college.

*Stephen Chbosky at a signing for the DVD release of* The Perks of Being a Wallflower, *in Los Angeles, Calif., Feb. 12, 2013.* Paul A. Herbert/Getty Images

Chbosky wrote and directed the 1995 film *The Four Corners of Nowhere*, which premiered at the Sundance Film Festival. In 1999, MTV Books published *The Perks of Being a Wallflower*, a novel Chbosky began writing in college. *The Perks of Being a Wallflower* is a coming-of-age story about a high school freshman named Charlie. The novel unfolds in a series of letters Charlie writes to an unnamed friend in which he describes his experiences of making friends, experimenting with drugs, exploring his sexuality, participating in screenings of *The Rocky Horror Picture Show* (film 1975), and coping with his friend's suicide. In addition to being a *New York Times* best seller, *The Perks of Being a Wallflower* has also been the subject of controversy. The book has been often criticized for its graphic depictions of homosexuality and drug use in a young adult novel. The American Library Association cites it as one of the most frequently challenged or banned books, although Chbosky claims he did not set out to write a controversial book. Chbosky directed the 2012 film adaption of the novel. He also wrote the screenplay for the film version of the popular musical *Rent* (film 2005) and the screenplay for the film adaptation of Michael Chabon's novel *The Mysteries of Pittsburgh* (1988, film 2008).

# SUZANNE COLLINS

## (b. 1962– )

U.S. children's book and television show writer Suzanne Collins was perhaps best known for her young adult science-fiction novels belonging to the Hunger Games trilogy. Since her book debut in the early 21st century, her work has become highly sought after by fans. Although some critics and general readers have pointed out that the violence in the Hunger Games series seems excessive for the intended audience, most critics have expressed mainly positive reviews.

Collins was born on Aug. 10, 1962, in Hartford, Conn. She graduated from Indiana University in 1985 with bachelor's degrees in telecommunications and in theater and drama. In the early 1990s she began writing for children's television on the Nickelodeon cable channel.

45

*Suzanne Collins.* © AP Images

She contributed to many shows, including *Clarissa Explains It All*, a teen sitcom that ran from 1991 to 1994, and *Oswald*, an animated series for preschoolers. Collins's interests then turned to books, and she decided to try writing one.

Collins first wrote a series of five books—collectively named the Underland

Chronicles—that were geared toward a middle-school audience. These fantasy books describe the adventures of Gregor, who lives below New York City with humans as well as with giant rats, spiders, bats, and other creatures. The books were published beginning in 2003 with *Gregor the Overlander* and ending in 2007 with *Gregor and the Code of Claw*. Collins's Hunger Games trilogy, consisting of *The Hunger Games* (2008), *Catching Fire* (2009), and *Mockingjay* (2010), were directed toward a teen audience. These sci-fi adventure books take place in a totalitarian world of the future, where each year a lottery picks two dozen teens to compete in a fight to the death. Blending themes of survival and power with those of social and economic division, all with political overtones, the books convey the journey of the protagonist as she searches for her identity in a dystopian world.

The three books of the Hunger Games trilogy were highly popular, and they all appeared as number one on the *New York Times* best-seller list. In 2012 the movie *The Hunger Games*, with Collins cowriting the screenplay and acting as a co-executive producer, was released.

# ROBERT CORMIER

(b. 1925–d. 2000)

R obert Cormier was an American author and journalist born on Jan. 17, 1925, in Leominster, Mass. Cormier wrote books for young adults that were both praised and criticized for their honesty and pessimism. He also wrote works of fiction for adults.

Robert Cormier worked as a radio writer and as a newspaper reporter beginning in the 1940s. He used the pseudonym John Fitch IV to write one of his newspaper columns. Cormier won awards from the New England Associated Press for news writing in 1959 and 1973. He wrote several novels for young adults, including *Now and at the Hour* (1960), *A Little Raw on Monday Mornings* (1963), *Take Me Where the Good Times Are* (1965), *The Chocolate War* (1974), *I Am the Cheese* (1977), and *After the First Death* (1979), as well as the short-story collection *Eight Plus One* (1980). Several of his books received the *New York Times* outstanding book of the year awards. One of these, *The Chocolate War,* tells of a high school student who is punished by both peers and faculty for his refusal to participate in a candy-selling fund-raiser for his school.

Cormier also wrote short stories and articles that appeared in such magazines as *Redbook*, the *Saturday Evening Post*, and *McCall's*. Unlike many writers for young adults, Cormier wrote realistic stories that focused more on external events and their effects on his characters than on simple personal struggles. Cormier was awarded an honorary doctor of letters degree from Fitchburg State College in 1977. His last work, *Frenchtown Summer*, was published in 1999. He died on Nov. 2, 2000, in Boston, Mass.

# CHRISTOPHER PAUL CURTIS

(b. 1953– )

The novel *Bud, Not Buddy* (1999) earned U.S. author Christopher Paul Curtis both the 2000 Newbery Medal and the Coretta Scott King Author Award. Curtis was the first writer to win both prestigious children's literature prizes in the same year.

Curtis was born on May 10, 1953, in Flint, Mich. After high school he worked at an auto plant for 13 years. Writing in a journal on his breaks helped Curtis deal with the monotony of the automobile assembly line. He later took classes part-time at the University of Michigan's Flint campus, earning his bachelor's degree in political science in 1996.

*Christopher Paul Curtis.* © AP Images

With the support of his wife and children, Curtis took a year off work to concentrate on writing. A manuscript he entered in a national contest impressed an editor from Delacorte Press, resulting in his first publication, *The Watsons Go to Birmingham—1963* (1995). The story of an African American family from Michigan that travels to the South to visit relatives in the summer of 1963, Curtis drew some of the inspiration from his own childhood and spent a great deal of time doing research in order to ensure historical accuracy. The publication was chosen as an honour book for both the Newbery and Coretta Scott King prizes, making it one of the most successful debut novels in the history of children's literature. Like his next work, *Bud, Not Buddy*—the story of an orphaned 10-year-old who runs away from a bad foster home during the Great Depression to search for his father—critics praised the book for its ability to appeal to readers of all ages and races, its interesting treatment of serious subject matter, and its entertaining characters.

Curtis's creative output continued into the 21st century. The modern-day fairy tale *Bucking the Sarge* (2004) is narrated by a teenaged boy whose mother, a selfish slum-lord, is called "the Sarge." *Mr. Chickee's Funny Money* (2005) details the adventures of an overachieving seven-year-old who aspires to become a detective. Curtis's next book, *Elijah of Buxton* (2007), follows a young slave who faces danger after escaping to Canada on the Underground Railroad. *The Mighty Miss Malone* (2012) is set during the Depression and centers on a 12-year-old girl who first appeared in *Bud, Not Buddy*.

# KAREN CUSHMAN

(b. 1941– )

U.S. author Karen Cushman burst onto the young adult fiction scene in the 1990s with several critically acclaimed his-torical novels that recreate in rich detail the lives and times of spirited, complex female protagonists.

Cushman was born on Oct. 4, 1941, in Chicago, Ill., but moved to southern California at age 11. Although she enjoyed reading and writing in her youth, she never seriously considered becoming a children's writer. She studied English and Greek at

*Karen Cushman.* Courtesy of Karen Cushman

Stanford University and received her bachelor's degree in 1963. After graduation, she held a variety of jobs, became a wife and mother, and later pursued a graduate degree in human behavior at United States International University. After earning a master's degree in museum studies at John F. Kennedy University in 1986, she joined the institution's staff as a teacher and editor.

Although she often told her family about ideas she had for stories, Cushman did not begin putting her thoughts down on paper until she was almost 50 years old. Her first book, *Catherine, Called Birdy*, was published in 1994. The book was set in the Middle Ages, and Cushman meticulously researched the period using a range of primary sources. She also studied the historical fiction of many well-known children's writers in order to get a better feel for writing for young adults. Written in diary format, the book chronicles the daily life of a teenager living in an English manor house with a mother intent on making her a proper lady and a father constantly attempting to marry her off. The coming-of-age story was chosen as a Newbery Honor Book in 1995 and won the Carl Sandburg Award for Children's Literature.

Cushman received the Newbery Medal the following year for *The Midwife's Apprentice* (1995). Although also set in the Middle Ages and involving a strong female lead character, this book centers on a homeless girl who gains purpose and confidence when she becomes the helper of a midwife who discovers her sleeping in a dung heap.

Cushman's third novel, *The Ballad of Lucy Whipple* (1996), takes place during the period of the California gold rush. The heroine learns about the true meaning of home when her family leaves Massachusetts for a new life in the West.

Cushman was honoured by numerous organizations, including the Society for Children's Book Writers and Illustrators, the Parent's Choice Foundation, and the American Booksellers Association. She has frequently visited schools to talk to youngsters about her books and career.

# SARAH DESSEN

(b. 1970– )

S arah Dessen is an American author of young adult novels whose works feature realistic protagonists struggling with the rapid changes and new situations that many teenagers face. Dessen's novels have earned her a dedicated following and numerous awards and recognitions.

Dessen was born on June 6, 1970 in Evanston, Ill., but grew up in Chapel Hill, N.C., where her parents were professors at the University of North Carolina, Chapel

*Sarah Dessen.* KPO Photo

Hill. Her father taught Shakespeare, and her mother taught classics. The literary atmosphere of her childhood was beneficial for Dessen as a young writer. She was an avid reader at an early age, and she began writing her own stories before she was ten years old. Dessen went to college at the University of North Carolina, where she focused on creative writing and graduated with a degree in English in 1993.

After college, Dessen decided to focus on writing novels instead of finding a more traditional job. After writing two novels that went unpublished, Dessen's third attempt, *That Summer*, was published in 1996. *That Summer* tells the story of Haven, a 15-year-old girl trying to cope with her father's remarriage to a younger woman, her sister's upcoming wedding, and the growth spurt that has made her into a gangly, five-foot-eleven teenager during a single summer. The novel was highly successful and well reviewed by critics. *That Summer* and Dessen's second novel, *Someone Like You* (1998), were the sources for the 2003 movie *How to Deal*. Dessen has since published many best-selling novels for teenagers, including *Just Listen* (2006), *Along for the Ride* (2009), and *What Happened to Goodbye* (2011). She has also

taught creative writing at the University of North Carolina, Chapel Hill.

# E.L. DOCTOROW

(b. 1931– )

O ne of the most distinguished modern American writers, E.L. Doctorow has won critical and popular acclaim for fiction produced in a range of prose styles, especially historical fiction. Edgar Laurence Doctorow was born in New York City on Jan. 6, 1931. He majored in philosophy at Kenyon College in Gambier, Ohio, graduating in 1952, then pursued graduate studies at Columbia University in New York City until 1953. After a two-year stint in the U.S. Army, Doctorow worked for Dial Press from 1964 to 1969 and then taught at various universities from 1971.

Among his novels are *Welcome to Hard Times* (1960); *The Book of Daniel* (1971); *Ragtime*, which won the 1976 National Book Critics Circle Award for fiction; and *Billy Bathgate*, which won that award in 1990. Doctorow also wrote the off-Broadway play *Drinks Before Dinner* (1978) and the screenplay for *Daniel* (1983), the film adaptation of his novel. Other novels include *The Waterworks* (1994) and *City of God* (2000). *The March* (2005) follows a fictionalized version of the Union general William Tecumseh Sherman on his infamously destructive trek through Georgia, aimed at weakening the Confederate economy, during the American Civil War. Doctorow's *Homer and Langley* (2009) mythologizes the lives of the Collyer brothers, a pair of reclusive eccentrics whose death in 1947 revealed a nightmarish collection of curiosities and garbage in their Harlem, New York City, brownstone. In 2012, Doctorow was the recipient of the PEN/Saul Bellow Award for Lifetime Achievement in American Fiction.

# RODDY DOYLE

(b. 1958– )

I rish author Roddy Doyle is known for his unvarnished depiction of the working class in Ireland. His distinctively Irish settings, style, mood, and phrasing have made him a favorite fiction writer in his own country as well as overseas.

The second of four children of a printer and a homemaker, Doyle was born on May

8, 1958, in Dublin, Ire. After majoring in English and geography at University College, Dublin, he taught those subjects for 14 years at Greendale Community School, a Dublin grade school. During the summer break of his third year of teaching, Doyle began writing seriously. The first editions of his comedic novel *The Commitments* (1987; film 1991) were published through his own company, King Farouk, until a London-based publisher took over. The work was the first installment of his internationally acclaimed Barrytown trilogy, which also included *The Snapper* (1990; film 1993) and *The Van* (1991; film 1996). The trilogy centers on the ups and downs of the never-say-die Rabbitte family, who temper the bleakness of life in an Irish slum with familial love and understanding.

Doyle's fourth novel, *Paddy Clarke Ha Ha Ha* (1993), won the 1993 Booker Prize. Set in the 1960s in a fictional working-class area of northern Dublin, the book examines the cruelty inflicted upon children by other children. The protagonist, 10-year-old Paddy Clarke, fears his classmates' ostracism, especially after the breakup of his parents' marriage. In mid-1994 Doyle launched the BBC miniseries *Family*, which generated heated controversy throughout conservative Ireland. The

*Roddy Doyle.* David Levenson/Getty Images

program shed harsh light on a family's struggle with domestic violence and alcoholism and portrayed the bleaker side of life in a housing project, the same venue he had used in his earlier Barrytown trilogy.

Doyle later wrote *The Woman Who Walked into Doors* (1997), a novel about domestic abuse; *A Star Called Henry* (1999), about an Irish Republican Army (IRA) soldier named Henry Smart and his adventures during the Easter Rising; *Oh, Play That Thing* (2004), which follows Smart as he journeys through America; and *The Dead Republic* (2010), the finale of the Henry Smart trilogy that shows him returning to Ireland and coming to grips with his troubling past in the IRA. Doyle's short-story collections include *The Deportees and Other Stories* (2008) and *Bullfighting* (2011).

# DAVE EGGERS

(b. 1970–)

Dave Eggers is an American author and publisher whose ambitious memoir *A Heartbreaking Work of Staggering Genius* (2000) established him as one of the most promising young writers of his generation. Eggers has since published numerous successful works of fiction and nonfiction. He is the founder and editor of the publishing house McSweeney's, and the cofounder of 826 Valencia, a nonprofit organization dedicated to helping under-privileged young people explore their creative potential through writing.

Dave Eggers was born on March 12, 1970, Boston, Mass., and grew up there as well as in Illinois, where he studied journalism at the University of Illinois at Urbana-Champaign. When both of his parents died within a very brief period, Eggers put his stud-ies on hold to help raise his eight-year-old brother, Christopher. The two moved to California, where Eggers struggled to get his literary career off the ground while raising "Toph." Egger relates his experiences dur-ing this period in his highly stylized memoir *A Heartbreaking Work of Staggering Genius.* It earned him instant acclaim and literary star-dom, as well as a Pulitzer Prize nomination.

Eggers has since produced numerous books, short stories, and screenplays. *What Is the What: The Autobiography of Valentino Achak Deng* (2006) fictionalizes the true story of a South Sudanese man who sur-vived the destruction of his family's village during Sudan's civil war and came to the

*Dave Eggers at the 2011 Sundance Film Festival, Park City, Utah.* George Pimentel/Getty Images

United States. In 2003, Eggers travelled with Valentino Achak Deng to South Sudan where, after a 17-year absence, they found his parents. *Zeitoun* (2009) is a nonfiction narrative about a Syrian American man's experiences in New Orleans after Hurricane Katrina. Eggers's novel *The Wild Things* (2009) is loosely based on Maurice Sendak's *Where the Wild Things Are*. Eggers also cowrote the screenplay for Spike Jonze's 2009 film *Where the Wild Things Are*. In the same year, the film *Away We Go*, which Eggers wrote with his wife, Vendela Vida, appeared on the big screen. Eggers's novel *A Hologram for the King* (2012) highlights contemporary concerns about outsourcing and globalization in the story of a middle-aged American salesman trying to get a business contract in Saudi Arabia.

Eggers founded McSweeney's publishing house, which started with the 1998 launch of the literary magazine *Timothy McSweeney's Quarterly Concern*. McSweeney's also publishes a wide range of fiction and nonfiction books, periodicals, and the DVD "magazine" *Wholphin*, which features new or relatively unknown short films.

In 2002, Eggers helped found the nonprofit organization 826 Valencia in San Francisco. The volunteer-based organization provides free tutoring and writing work-shops that encourage kids' creativity and love of books. When branches of 826 Valencia opened in other major cities, including Chicago, Seattle, and New York, the organization became known as 826 National. The organization also helps its students get funding for college through its ScholarMatch program.

Dave Eggers was the youngest-ever recipient of the Heinz Family Foundation arts and humanities award for his contributions not only to literature but also to the writing community.

# BUCHI EMECHETA

## (b. 1944– )

E mecheta is an Igbo writer whose novels deal largely with the difficult and unequal role of women in both immigrant and African societies.

Born July 21, 1944 in Lagos, Nig., Emecheta was married at age 16 and immigrated with her husband to London in 1962. The problems she encountered in London during the early 1960s provided background for the books that are called her immigrant novels. Her first two books, *In the Ditch* (1972) and *Second-Class Citizen* (1974)—both later included in the single volume *Adah's Story* (1983)—introduce Emecheta's three major themes: the quests for equal treatment, self-confidence, and dignity as a woman. Somewhat different in style, Emecheta's later novel *Gwendolen* (1989; also published as *The Family*) also addresses the issues of immigrant life in Great Britain.

Most of Emecheta's other novels—including *The Bride Price* (1976), *The Slave Girl* (1977), *The Joys of Motherhood* (1979), *Destination Biafra* (1982), and *Double Yoke* (1982)—are realistic novels set in Africa that explore Emecheta's favourite themes. Perhaps her strongest work, *The Rape of Shavi* (1983), is also the most difficult to categorize. Set in an imaginary idyllic African kingdom, it gives an account of the events that occur when European refugees from a nuclear disaster arrive.

Emecheta also wrote an autobiography, *Head Above Water* (1986), and several works of children's and juvenile fiction.

# SID FLEISCHMAN

(b. 1920–d. 2010)

From the tall tales of his McBroom books to the comedic escapades of his 1987 Newbery winner *The Whipping Boy*, humor has played a key role in U.S. author Sid Fleischman's success as a children's writer. Several of Fleischman's books have been made into films.

Albert Sidney Fleischman was born on March 16, 1920, in Brooklyn, N.Y., but grew up in California. After touring as a professional magician from 1938 to 1941, Fleischman served in the United States Naval Reserve from 1941 to 1945. He received a bachelor's degree from San Diego State College (now University) in 1949 and held local reporting and editing jobs before becoming a full-time writer in 1951.

Fleischman became a published author in 1948 with *The Straw Donkey Case*, an adult mystery. He continued to write novels for adults throughout the 1950s and early 1960s. He received critical acclaim for *Mr. Mysterious and Company* (1962), which marked his juvenile literature debut.

Fleischman first introduced the character of McBroom in *McBroom Tells the Truth*, published in 1966. He created new adventures for the character throughout the next decades and became known as a master of tall tales. The Society of Children's Book Writers honoured Fleischman with a Golden Kite award in 1974 for *McBroom the Rainmaker* (1973).

Fleischman frequently combined his interest in history and folklore with his love of adventure and humour, as in *The Ghost in the Noonday Sun* (1965) and *Chancy and the Grand Rascal* (1966). Perhaps the best-known example of this genre is *The Whipping Boy* (1986), a story that evolved from Fleischman learning about the old practice of a boy being kept in royal households to receive the punishment for the prince's bad behavior. Fleischman takes the aptly named Prince Brat and his companion outside the castle, where they meet colourful characters and discover things about the world and each other while escaping problematic situations.

Among Fleischman's other children's books were *Me and the Man on the Moon-Eyed Horse* (1977), *Humbug Mountain*

*Sid Fleishman.* Kevin O'Malley

(1978), and *The Midnight Horse* (1990). His biographies written for children include: *Escape!: The Story of the Great Houdini* (2006) and *The Trouble Begins at 8: A Life of Mark Twain in the Wild, Wild West* (2008). Several of his books were adapted into movies, including *By the Great Horn Spoon!* (1963), which Disney released as *Bullwhip Griffin* (1967). Fleischman's screenwriting credits included *Blood Alley* (1955), *Scalawag* (1973), and the television show *3-2-1 Contact* (1979–82). His son Paul also is a Newbery-winning author. Fleischman died March 17, 2010, in Santa Monica, Calif.

# PAULA FOX

(b. 1923– )

U.S. author and educator Paula Fox was born on April 22, 1923, in New York City. Her work has been praised for its straightforward writing style that belies the turmoil below the surface. Her keen insight into the way people relate to one another and to themselves elevated her novels to a level above most popular fiction.

Growing up, Fox studied at schools in New York, New Hampshire, Montreal, and Cuba, before going on to Columbia University. She also studied piano at the Juilliard School and worked as a news reporter in Europe before beginning a teaching career at the State University of New York in 1963. Fox won a National Institute of Arts and Letters Award in 1972 and was a Guggenheim fellow in the same year. She wrote both children's books and books for adults. Her children's books included *Maurice's Room* (1966), *How Many Miles to Babylon?* (1967), *Portrait of Ivan* (1969), *Blowfish Live in the Sea* (1970), *The Western Coast* (1972), *The Slave Dancer* (1973), and *The Little Swineherd and Other Tales* (1978). *Poor George* (1967) and *Desperate Characters* (1970) were two of her adult novels.

*The Slave Dancer* won the 1974 Newbery Medal, and in 1978 Fox was awarded a Hans Christian Andersen Medal for all of her children's books. Her novel *Desperate Characters*, which examines the married life and relationships of Sophie and Otto, was made into a motion picture in 1970. Her energetic writing style is evident in all of her books. Isolation and the difficulty of communication between people, especially between children and adults, are also themes Fox has used in many of her novels.

# NADINE GORDIMER

(b. 1923– )

The South African novelist and short-story writer Nadine Gordimer has often written on themes of exile and alienation. She received the Nobel Prize for Literature in 1991.

Gordimer was born in Springs, Transvaal, South Africa, on Nov. 20, 1923, into a privileged, white, middle-class family. By the age of 9 she was writing, and she published her first story in a magazine when she was 15. Never an outstanding scholar, she attended the University of Witwatersrand for one year. Her wide reading, however, informed her about the world on the other side of apartheid—the official South African policy of racial segregation—and that discovery in time developed into strong political opposition to apartheid. She became a longtime member of the African National Congress, and because of her political views her books were banned in her country from 1958 to 1991. In addition to writing, she lectured

and taught at various schools in the United States during the 1960s and 1970s.

Gordimer's fiction concerns the devastating effects of apartheid on the lives of South Africans. She examines how public events affect individual lives, how the dreams of one's youth are corrupted, and how innocence is lost. Her first book, a collection of short stories entitled *The Soft Voice of the Serpent*, appeared in 1952. The next year a novel, *The Lying Days*, was published. Both exhibit the clear, controlled, and unsentimental technique that became her hallmark. Her novel *The Conservationist* (1974) won the Booker Prize in 1974. Later works include *Burger's Daughter* (1979), *July's People* (1981), *A Sport of Nature* (1987), *My Son's Story* (1990), *None to Accompany Me* (1994), and *The House Gun* (1998).

Gordimer addressed environmental issues in *Get a Life* (2005), the story of a South African ecologist who, after receiving thyroid treatment, becomes radioactive to others. *No Time Like the Present* (2012) follows veterans of the battle against apartheid as they deal with the issues facing modern South Africa. She also wrote a number of short-story collections, including *A Soldier's Embrace* (1980), *Crimes of Conscience* (1991), and *Loot and Other Stories* (2003). *Living in Hope and History: Notes from Our Century* (1999) is a collection of essays, correspondence, and reminiscences. In 2007 Gordimer was awarded the French Legion of Honour.

# GÜNTER GRASS

(b. 1927– )

The German poet, novelist, and playwright Günter Grass served as the literary spokesman for the German generation that grew up in the Nazi era. In 1999 he was awarded the Nobel Prize for Literature.

Günter Wilhelm Grass was born in Danzig (now Gdansk), Pol., on Oct. 16, 1927. He passed through the Hitler Youth movement, was drafted at 16, was wounded in battle, and became a prisoner of war. Later, while an art student in Düsseldorf, he supported himself as a dealer in the black market, a tombstone cutter, and a drummer in a jazz band. Encouraged by the writers' association Gruppe 47, he produced poems and plays, at first with little success.

In 1956 Grass went to Paris and wrote *Die Blechtrommel* (1959; film 1979; *The Tin Drum*).

This exuberant, picaresque novel, written in a variety of styles, imaginatively distorts and exaggerates his personal experiences—the Polish-German dualism of Danzig, the creeping Nazification of average families, the attrition of the war years, the coming of the Russians, and the complacent atmosphere of West Germany's postwar "economic miracle." It was followed by *Katz und Maus* (1961; *Cat and Mouse*) and an epic novel, *Hundejahre* (1963; *Dog Years*). The three books together form a trilogy set in Danzig.

Grass's other novels were always politically topical. *Örtlich Betäubt* (1969; *Local Anaesthetic*) is a protest against the Vietnam War. *Der Butt* (1977; *The Flounder*) is a ribald fable of the war between the sexes from the Stone Age to the present. *Das Treffen in Telgte* (1979; *The Meeting at Telgte*) tells of a hypothetical "Gruppe 1647" meeting of authors at the close of the Thirty Years' War. In *Kopfgeburten: oder die Deutschen sterben aus* (1980; *Headbirths: or, the Germans Are Dying Out*), Grass describes a young couple's agonizing over whether to have a child in the face of a population explosion and the threat of nuclear war. *Unkenrufe* (1992; *The Call of the Toad*) concerns the uneasy relationship between Poland and Germany.

*Günter Grass.* Sean Gallup/Getty Images

In 1995 Grass published *Ein weites Feld* (*A Broad Field*), an ambitious novel treating Germany's reunification in 1990. The work was attacked by German critics, who denounced Grass's portrayal of reunification as "misconstrued" and "unreadable." Grass, whose leftist political views were often not well received, was outspoken in his belief that Germany lacked "the politically organized power to renew itself." *Mein Jahrhundert* (1999; *My Century*), a collection of 100 related stories, was less overtly political than many of his earlier works. In it Grass relates the events of the 20th century using a story for each year, each with a different narrator.

Grass was a longtime participant in Social Democratic party politics in West Berlin, fighting for social and literary causes. When he was awarded the Nobel Prize for Literature in 1999, there were many who believed that his strong, and sometimes unpopular, political beliefs had prevented him from receiving the prize sooner. Grass's disclosure of his membership in the Waffen-SS, which came just before publication of his memoir *Beim Häuten der Zwiebel* (2006; *Peeling the Onion*), caused widespread controversy, with some arguing that it undercut his moral authority. He had previously claimed that he had been drafted into an air defense unit in 1944. *Unterwegs von Deutschland nach Deutschland: Tagebuch 1990* (2009; *From Germany to Germany: Diary 1990*) was a diary of his experiences in East and West Germany during the period between the fall of the Berlin Wall and reunification. Grass wrote two more volumes of autobiography, *Die Box* (2008; *The Box*) and *Grimms Wörter: eine Liebeserklärung* (2010; *Grimms' Words: A Declaration of Love*), the latter of which explores Grass's political past through a loving analysis of the Brothers Grimm.

# JOHN GREEN

### (b. 1977– )

John Green is an American author of sophisticated young adult fiction. His best-selling novels have won numerous awards, including the Printz Award for his first novel *Looking for Alaska* (2005).

Green was born Aug. 24, 1977, in Indianapolis, Ind. He lived most of his childhood in Orlando, Fla., and went to college at Kenyon University, where he double-majored in English and religious studies. After graduating in 2000, Green worked as a chaplain

at a children's hospital before taking a job at *Booklist* magazine, where he worked as a production editor and book reviewer. Green has since contributed radio scripts for WBEZ in Chicago and National Public Radio's *All Things Considered.*

*Looking for Alaska* is a coming-of-age novel that tells the story of Miles "Pudge" Halter, a 16-year-old boy whose previously uneventful life is turned upside down when he leaves Florida to attend boarding school in Birmingham, Alabama. There, Miles befriends a group of smart and vibrant but rowdy students, including Alaska, a wild young girl with whom Miles falls in love. Green's own experiences at boarding school influenced the novel, which was highly praised for its realistic depiction of the excitement and intensity of teenage life. Green has since written a number of novels for young adults, including *An Abundance of Katherines* (2006), *Paper Towns* (2008), *Will Grayson, Will Grayson* (cowritten with David Levithan, 2009), and *The Fault in Our Stars* (2012), which *Time* magazine named one of the ten best fiction books of 2012.

In addition to fiction writing, Green is an active blogger. He and his brother upload two videos per week to their YouTube channel, VlogBrothers. The YouTube channel

*John Green.* Ton Koene/Gamma-Rapho/Getty Images

has served as the platform for a number of charitable projects to "decrease the overall worldwide level of suck."

# ROSA GUY

(b. 1922–d. 2012)

Rosa Guy was an American writer who drew on her own experiences to create fiction for young adults that usually concerned individual choice, family conflicts, poverty, and the realities of life in urban America and the West Indies.

Guy was born Rosa Cuthbert on Sept. 1, 1922 in Trinidad, West Indies. Cuthbert lived in Trinidad until 1932, when she moved to the United States to join her parents, who had already immigrated. She grew up in New York City's Harlem. At age 14, after both of her parents died, she was compelled to go to work in a factory, and in 1941 she married Walter Guy. She eventually studied writing at New York University and became active in the American Negro Theatre. In the late 1940s, after her marriage ended, Guy cofounded the Harlem Writers Guild and focused on her fiction.

Guy's first novel, *Bird at My Window* (1966), is set in Harlem and examines the relationship between black mothers and their children, as well as the social forces that can foster the demoralization of black men. *Children of Longing* (1970), which Guy edited, contains accounts of black teens' and young adults' firsthand experiences and aspirations. After the publication of these works, she traveled in the Caribbean and lived in Haiti and Trinidad. Guy became best known for a frank coming-of-age trilogy that featured *The Friends* (1973), *Ruby* (1976), and *Edith Jackson* (1978). She also wrote a number of books featuring Imamu Jones, a young African American detective in Harlem; the series included *The Disappearance* (1979), *New Guys Around the Block* (1983), and *And I Heard a Bird Sing* (1987). Among her other works are *A Measure of Time* (1983), *Paris, Pee Wee, and Big Dog* (1984), *My Love, My Love; or, The Peasant Girl* (1985, on which the successful 1990 Broadway musical *Once on This Island* was based), *The Ups and Downs of Carl David III* (1989), *Billy the Great* (1991), and *The Music of Summer* (1992). *The Sun, the Sea, a Touch of the Wind* (1995) is a novel for adults about an American artist living in Haiti who reexamines her troubled past. Guy died June 3, 2012, in New York, N.Y.

# CARL HIAASEN

(b. 1953– )

C arl Hiaasen is an American investigative reporter and novelist from Florida whose razor-sharp works often cut to the heart of his home state's social problems, such as government corruption, environmental crime, and drug smuggling. Best known for his journalism and satiric crime fiction for adults, Hiaasen has also written a number of children's books, including *Hoot* (2002), which won a Newbery Honor Award in 2003.

Hiaasen was born March 12, 1953, in Fort Lauderdale, Fla. Growing up in south Florida, Hiaasen loved spending time outside in the state's natural environment. Soon after graduating from the University of Florida's College of Journalism and Communication in 1974, Hiaasen was hired as a reporter for the *Miami Herald* and eventually joined the newspaper's investigative reporting team. Hiaasen has written his own weekly column for the paper since 1985, writing on topics such as political scandals, ecological issues, and the government's incompetence.

Hiaasen's experience in journalism helped him develop the writing style and subject matter that make up his fiction. Hiaasen published his first novel *Powder Burn*—cowritten with the journalist Bill Montalbano—in 1981. The novel is a tightly plotted crime thriller about an innocent man who finds himself entangled with Miami, Florida's cocaine trade and a corrupt police force after witnessing a murder. Hiaasen wrote two more novels with Montalbano before striking out on his own with his 1986 novel, *Tourist Season*. Couched in Hiaasen's characteristic humor, *Tourist Season* tells the story of a conspiracy by environmentalists to save Florida's ecosystem by terrorizing tourists. Hiaasen has since published many novels, including the *New York Times* best seller *Striptease* (1993), which was made into a 1996 film starring Demi Moore, and the 2013 *Bad Monkey*, a humorous crime novel featuring a wide array of colourful and ever-surprising Floridians.

Hiaasen's *Hoot*, published in 2002, makes his environmentalist concerns accessible to younger readers. The book was both critically acclaimed and immensely popular, spending over two years on the *New York Time*'s bestseller list. The American singer-songwriter Jimmy Buffet liked the book and coproduced the 2006 film adaptation. Hiaasen has since written three other novels for young people: *Flush* (2005), *Scat* (2009), and *Chomp* (2012).

In addition to his novels, Hiaasen has produced several nonfiction works, including two collections taken from his newspaper columns, *Kick Ass* (1999) and *Paradise Screwed* (2001). *Team Rodent: How Disney Devours the World* (1998) is an entertaining yet serious argument against the cultural and economic power of the Walt Disney Company. With *The Downhill Lie: A Hacker's Return to a Ruinous Sport* (2008), Hiaasen reflects on his relationship with his father as he recounts his frustrations on the golf course.

# S.E. HINTON

(b. 1950– )

Susan Eloise Hinton was born on July 22, 1950, in Tulsa, Okla. As a young writer, Hinton decided to write under her initials in order to deflect attention from her gender. She set out to write about the difficult social system that teenagers create among themselves. Her books struck a chord with readers who saw in her characters many

*Carl Hiaasen during the April 2006 Los Angeles premiere of* Hoot. M. Phillips/WireImage/Getty Images

elements of this system that existed in their own schools and towns.

In 1967, while she was still in high school, a friend's mother helped the then 16-year-old Hinton publish her first book, *The Outsiders*. The story of confrontation between two rival groups of teenagers was immediately successful with critics and young readers, and it won several awards. There was some controversy about the level of violence in the novel and in her other works, but Hinton was praised for her realistic and explosive dialogue. *The Outsiders*, which remains her most famous, successful, and best-loved novel, enabled Hinton to continue her education in college.

Hinton graduated from the University of Tulsa in 1970. Her other novels for young adults included *That Was Then, This Is Now* (1971), *Rumble Fish* (1975), *Tex* (1979), and *Taming the Star Runner* (1988). Each of her books featured a cast of characters that suffered from society's ills. Young people alienated from their families and from their peers were seen to veer into criminal paths. Several of her books, including *The Outsiders* and *Rumble Fish*, were later adapted as motion pictures.

In the 1990s Hinton wrote *Big David, Little David* and *The Puppy Sister* for younger readers. She published *Hawkes Harbor*, a novel for adults, in 2004.

# ANTHONY HOROWITZ

(b. 1955– )

P rolific English author Anthony Horowitz is equally adept at writing novels, plays, television shows, and films. He is well known for his popular young adult fiction, including the series starring boy spy Alex Rider, as well as the Power of Five series, which involves teenage characters who possess superpowers. Horowitz has created and written several television shows that were originally telecast in Great Britain but have since been shown in other countries.

Horowitz was born on April 5, 1955, in London, Eng. After deciding at an early age that he wanted to be a writer, he attended the University of York to further that goal. He published his first book, *The Sinister Secret of Frederick K. Bower* (also published as *Enter Frederick K. Bower*), a children's adventure story, in 1979. In the early 1980s Horowitz

concentrated on writing books for the Pentagram series, which included *The Devil's Door-bell* (1983), *The Night of the Scorpion* (1985), *The Silver Citadel* (1986), and *Day of the Dragon* (1989). These science-fiction books revolve around characters who fight against an evil that threatens the world. The books did not sell well, however, and Horowitz never wrote the fifth and final story of the series.

In the 1980s Horowitz also began his Diamond Brothers series, which relates humorous stories about an inept 20-something private detective and his teen-age sibling who actually solves the cases. Aiming for a preteen or young teen audience, this series includes both full-length novels and shorter novellas with titles such as *The Falcon's Malteser* (1986), *South by South East* (1991), and *The Greek Who Stole Christmas* (2007). The first book appeared as a television show, *Just Ask for Diamond*, in 1988. Simultaneously, Horowitz published *Groosham Grange* (1988), about a teenage witch who is unhappy at boarding school. In 1999 a sequel, *The Unholy Grail* (republished as *Return to Groosham Grange*, 2003), was published.

Horowitz began the 21st century by releasing the first of his Alex Rider novels. This series starts with the main character, a

*Anthony Horowitz.* Courtesy of Walker Books Ltd.

14-year-old boy, being blackmailed into joining MI6, the British Secret Intelligence Service. Each book places Alex in dangerous yet thrilling spy situations. The first book in the series, *Stormbreaker* (2000), was made into a movie titled *Alex Rider: Operation Stormbreaker* in 2006, with Horowitz writing the screenplay. Other titles in the Alex Rider book series include *Eagle Strike* (2003), *Snakehead* (2007), and *Scorpia Rising: The Final Mission* (2011).

Beginning in 2005, Horowitz started publishing books for the Power of Five series (called the Gatekeepers in the United States). These novels were updated, revamped versions of the Pentagram series. Starring five teenagers trying to save the world from being destroyed, these books blended pulse-pounding action sequences reminiscent of the Alex Rider series with supernatural elements including witches and demons. The Power of Five books, which began with *Raven's Gate* (2005) and ended with *Oblivion* (2012), gained popular and critical acclaim.

In addition to his young adult novels, Horowitz is an accomplished writer in other genres. He was involved with numerous television shows since the 1980s, most notably the murder mystery *Murder in Mind*, the crime drama *Collision*, and the detective drama *Foyle's*

*War*, all produced in the early 21st century. His horror film, *The Gathering*, starring U.S. actress Christina Ricci, was released in 2002, and his play, *Mindgame* (2000), debuted in New York City in 2008.

# KHALED HOSSEINI

(b. 1965– )

Hosseini is an Afghan-born American novelist known for his vivid depictions of Afghanistan, most notably in *The Kite Runner* (2003).

Born March 4, 1965, in Kabul, Afg., Hosseini grew up in Kabul; his father was a diplomat and his mother a secondary-school teacher. In 1976 he and his parents moved to Paris, where his father worked at the Afghan embassy. With the Soviet invasion of Afghanistan in 1979, the family found returning to their home impossible, and they moved to California, having been granted political asylum by the United States. Hosseini attended Santa Clara University, where he studied biology, and in 1989 he began attending medical school at the University of California, San Diego. He entered private

practice as an internist in 1996, three years after receiving his medical degree.

Hosseini began working in 2001 on *The Kite Runner*, writing at 4:00 AM before heading to his medical practice. The novel's narrator is Amir, a writer who lives in California in the present day but who grew up in the 1970s in Kabul, the privileged son of a wealthy family. Amir's story features his childhood friendship with Hassan, the son of a family servant, and its subsequent dissolution. *The Kite Runner* was praised for its powerful storytelling, but it was, at times, dismissed by critics for elements considered melodramatic. Nonetheless, the novel soon gained wide popularity through readers' word-of-mouth praise, and it was eventually published in more than three dozen countries; a film adaptation was released in 2007. Prompted by this success, Hosseini turned to writing full-time in 2004. The focus brought by the novel to the continuing Afghan refugee crisis led to his appointment as a goodwill envoy for the UN High Commissioner for Refugees in 2006.

Hosseini's second novel, *A Thousand Splendid Suns* (2007), was inspired by his observations of women wearing burkas during a 2003 visit to Afghanistan, his first trip there since childhood. Continuing in the topical vein of *The Kite Runner*, the book depicts the radical shifts in the political and social climate of Afghanistan through the relation-ship between two women, Mariam and Laila, the first and second wives of an abusive husband. His third novel, *And the Mountains Echoed* (2013), spanning nearly 60 years of Afghan history, is a saga about family, loss, and love.

# EVAN HUNTER

(b. 1926–d. 2005)

Among the best-selling fiction of prolific U.S. writer Evan Hunter were more than 50 crime stories published under the pseud-onym Ed McBain. Hunter also published under the names Curt Cannon, Ezra Hannon, Hunt Collins, and Richard Marsten.

Hunter was born Salvatore A. Lombino on Oct. 15, 1926, in New York City. He graduated from Hunter College in 1950 and held various short-term jobs, including playing piano in a jazz band and teaching in vocational high schools, while writing his early stories. His best-known novel is among his earliest: *The Blackboard Jungle* (1954), a story of violence in a New York high school that was the basis of a popular film (1955). After his *Strangers When We Meet* (1958; filmed 1960) and *A Matter of Conviction* (1959; published in the United States as *The Young Savages*) became best sellers, Hunter wrote the screenplays for both (1960–61), as well as for Alfred Hitchcock's *The Birds* (1962) and several later films. Hunter wrote several novels on the theme of family tensions between generations, including *Mothers and Daughters* (1961), *Last Summer* (1968; film 1969), *Sons* (1969), and *Streets of Gold* (1974).

Hunter was most prolific as a crime novelist. Nearly all of his McBain books are novels of police procedure set in the 87th Precinct of a city much like New York. They include *Cop Hater* (1956; film 1958), *Fuzz* (1968; film 1972), *Widows* (1991), and *Mischief* (1993). Hunter also wrote children's stories and stage plays. His later works include *Criminal Conversation* (1994), *Privileged Conversation* (1996), and *Me and Hitch* (1997). Hunter died on July 6, 2005, in Weston, Conn.

# JOHN IRVING

(b. 1942– )

U sing a mix of humour and despair, U.S. author John Irving is known for his lengthy novels in which he explores rules of behavior and the consequences of breaking social codes. Irving's stories are full of oddball characters entangled in comically convoluted plots. Beginning with his breakthrough novel, *The World According to Garp* (1978), Irving achieved both literary and celebrity stature while engaging readers with a string of international best sellers.

John Wallace Blunt, Jr., was born on March 2, 1942, in Exeter, N.H., to parents who divorced before his birth. He was renamed John Winslow Irving at age six, when his mother remarried and his stepfather adopted him; he never knew his biological father. He attended Phillips Exeter Academy, where he took up wrestling, which would remain a lifelong passion, struggling academically because of dyslexia. Following his graduation in 1962, he spent time at the Universities of Pittsburgh and Vienna before receiving a bachelor's degree in English from the University of New Hampshire (1965) and a master's degree in

English from the University of Iowa (1967). From 1967 to 1978 Irving taught at a number of colleges and universities, including Windham College, the University of Iowa Writer's Workshop, Mount Holyoke College, and Brandeis University.

Irving's early novels, which earned praise but poor sales, were published during his years in academia. Set in Austria, *Setting Free the Bears* (1969) told of a group of pranksters intent on liberating the inhabitants of the Vienna Zoo. *The Water-Method Man* (1972) dealt with the chaotic life of a rogue named Fred Bogus Trumper. *The 158-Pound Marriage* (1974) questioned the viability of the institution of marriage.

Irving continued teaching until 1978, when his fourth novel, *The World According to Garp*, achieved a rare combination of wide readership and literary acclaim, giving him the opportunity to write full-time. The novel chronicled the life of the novelist T.S. Garp from conception to death through a narrative populated with eccentrics and the violent events that befall them. Although the fates of its characters are often tragic, *Garp* was almost universally regarded as a comic novel because of the way in which the events are filtered through Garp's unique imagination. The book's phenomenal success transformed Irving into one of America's foremost celebrity authors. A film adaptation, released in 1982, contributed to the novel's enduring popularity.

The novels that followed Garp variously recalled their predecessor in form and

*John Irving.* Cesar Rangel/AFP/Getty Images

subject matter. *The Hotel New Hampshire* (1981) told the story of an eccentric, disaster-prone family that sets up house in unlikely hotels in the United States and abroad. *The Cider House Rules* (1985) centered on an orphanage where doctors familiar with the dismal conditions of the place performed illegal abortions out of a sense of compassion. *A Prayer for Owen Meany* (1989) was a novel of religious revelation in a small New England town.

Following the publication of *Trying to Save Peggy Sneed* (1993), a collection of memoirs, short fiction, and literary essays, Irving released his next novel, *A Son of the Circus*, in 1994, followed by *A Widow for One Year* in 1998.

Although Irving consistently enjoyed worldwide commercial success following the publication of *Garp*, critical response to his work was mixed. Frequent points of contention were his often improbable story lines and his supposed fascination with the bizarre, which earned him a reputation as a writer whose primary concern was entertainment. Irving countered by insisting that his characters and the randomness of their fates only reflected the unpredictability, and danger, of ordinary life.

# THOMAS KENEALLY

(b. 1935– )

K nown for his historical novels, Australian author Thomas Keneally has often written about characters gripped by their historical and personal pasts. His moving work *Schindler's Ark,* based on a true story of the Holocaust, was adapted into the Academy Award–winning film *Schindler's List* in 1993.

Keneally was born on Oct. 7, 1935, in Sydney, Australia. At age 17 he entered a Roman Catholic seminary, but he left before ordination. His seminary experience influenced his early fiction, including *The Place at Whitton* (1964) and *Three Cheers for the Paraclete* (1968). Keneally established a reputation as a historical novelist with *Bring Larks and Heroes* (1967), about Australia's early years as an English penal colony. Keneally won international acclaim with the novel *The Chant of Jimmie Blacksmith* (1972), which is based on a true story of a half-caste Aboriginal who rebels against white racism by going on a murder spree.

Although Australia has figured promi-nently in much of Keneally's work, his range is broad. His well-received *Gossip from the*

*Forest* (1975) examines the World War I armistice through the eyes of a thoughtful, humane German negotiator. He was praised also for his treatment of the American Civil War in *Confederates* (1979). His best-known work, *Schindler's Ark* (1982; also published as *Schindler's List*), tells the story of Oskar Schindler, a German industrialist who saved more than 1,300 Jews from the Nazis. Controversy surrounded the book's receipt of the Booker Prize; detractors argued that the work was mere historical reporting. Keneally's later fiction includes *A Family Madness* (1985), *To Asmara* (1989), *Flying Hero Class* (1991), *Woman of the Inner Sea* (1992), *Jacko* (1993), *Homebush Boy* (1995), *The Great Shame* (1998), *Bettany's Book* (2000), *The Tyrant's Novel* (2003), *The Widow and Her Hero* (2007), and *The Daughters of Mars* (2012).

# BARBARA KINGSOLVER

(b. 1955– )

Barbara Kingsolver is an American writer and political activist whose best-known novels concern the endurance of people living in often inhospitable environments and the beauty to be found even in such harsh circumstances.

Born April 8, 1955, in Annapolis, Md., Kingsolver grew up in eastern Kentucky, the daughter of a physician who treated the rural poor. After graduating from DePauw University in Greencastle, Ind., she traveled and worked in Europe and then returned to the United States.

Kingsolver's novel *The Bean Trees* (1988) concerns a woman who makes a meaningful life for herself and a young Cherokee girl with whom she moves from rural Kentucky to the Southwest. In *Animal Dreams* (1990) a disconnected woman finds purpose and moral challenges when she returns to live in her small Arizona hometown. *Pigs in Heaven* (1993), a sequel to her first novel, deals with the main character's attempts to defend her adoption of her Native American daughter. Kingsolver's short-story collection, *Homeland and Other Stories*, was released in 1989. *Another America* (*Otra America*) (1991), a poetry collection in English, with a Spanish translation, primarily concerns the struggles of impoverished women against sexual and political abuse, war, and death.

With *The Poisonwood Bible* (1999), Kingsolver expanded her psychic and geographic territory, setting her story about the redemption of a missionary family in the Belgian Congo during the colony's struggle for independence. In *Prodigal Summer* (2001) the intertwined lives of several characters living in Appalachia highlight the relationship between humans and the natural world. Her next novel, *The Lacuna* (2009), combines history and fiction as it traces the life of a Mexican American novelist who befriends artist Frida Kahlo and communist leader Leon Trotsky and who is later investigated during the anticommunist McCarthy era. In 2010 *The Lacuna* won the Orange Prize for Fiction. A global warming story set in Appalachia, *Flight Behavior* (2012) details a community's reactions to the astonishing arrival of thousands of monarch butterflies, which have forgone their winter migration because of warming temperatures in northern climates.

Kingsolver also wrote the nonfictional *Holding the Line: Women in the Great Arizona Mine Strike of 1983* (1989), which records the endeavours of a group of women fighting the repressive policies of a mining corporation. Essay collections such as *High Tide in Tucson: Essays from Now or Never* (1995)

*Winner of the 2010 Orange Prize for Fiction, Barbara Kingsolver reacts after receiving the award for her book* The Lacuna. **Alastair Grant/AFP/Getty Images**

and *Small Wonder* (2002) contain observations on nature, family life, and world events. In *Animal, Vegetable, Miracle* (2007), Kingsolver writes about the environmental consequences of human consumption, using anecdotes from her own experiences eating only locally grown food to propose an alternate means of subsistence.

# STIEG LARSSON

(b. 1954–d. 2004)

S tieg Larsson was a Swedish writer and activist whose Millennium series of crime novels, published after his 2004 death, brought him international fame and praise.

Born Aug. 15, 1954, in Skelleftehamn, Swe., Larsson grew up with his maternal grandparents in northern Sweden until he was nine, when he rejoined his parents in Stockholm. As a teenager he wrote constantly and, inspired by his grandfather's strong antifascist beliefs, developed an interest in radical leftwing politics. Following 14 months of mandatory service in the Swedish army, Larsson participated

in rallies against the Vietnam War and
became involved in a revolutionary communist group. In 1977, after traveling to
Ethiopia, he worked as a graphic designer

*Stieg Larsson.* Scanpix Sweden/Claudio Bresciani/
AP Images

for a Swedish news agency, where he later worked as a journalist as well and would remain for 22 years. He also wrote articles for a British magazine that investigated and exposed fascism.

Larsson had become a respected journalist and an expert on the activities of those involved in extreme right-wing movements in Sweden by the 1990s. In 1991 he cowrote (with Anna-Lena Lodenius) a book on the subject, *Extremhögern* ("The Extreme Right"). Four years later, in response to the rising tide of neo-Nazism in Sweden, he helped establish the Expo Foundation—an organization dedicated to studying racist and antidemocratic tendencies in society in an effort to counteract them—also serving as editor in chief of its *Expo* magazine. As one of his country's most vocal opponents of hate groups, he became a frequent target of death threats.

Larsson started to write fiction in 2001 as a means of making more money. Influenced by the detective novels of English-language writers such as Elizabeth George and Sara Paretsky, he conceived a 10-volume series of thrillers in which a disgraced journalist pairs with a young tech-savvy misfit to uncover a host of crimes and conspiracies. When Larsson contacted a publisher in 2003, he had already written two novels, and he later completed a third; the following year, however, he suffered a fatal heart attack.

The first book in the series, *Män som hatar kvinnor* (2005; "Men Who Hate Women"; Eng. trans. *The Girl with the Dragon Tattoo*), which tracked the mismatched main characters' investigation into a decades-old disappearance, was swiftly met with praise in Sweden. Its two sequels—*Flickan som lekte med elden* (2006; *The Girl Who Played with Fire*) and *Luftslottet som sprängdes* (2007; "The Air Castle That Blew Up"; Eng trans. *The Girl Who Kicked the Hornets' Nest*)—earned similar acclaim. Though some critics charged that the novels' focus on violence against women was complicated by graphic depictions of such violence, the books became extremely popular both within and outside Sweden. Together, Larsson's novels were translated into over 30 languages and sold tens of million copies worldwide. A Swedish film adaptation of the series was produced in 2009, and an English-language film of the first novel was released two years later.

# KATHRYN LASKY

(b. 1944–)

Kathryn Lasky is an American author of more than one hundred children's books, nonfiction books, and novels for young people and adults. An enormously versatile writer, Lasky has written fiction and nonfiction works on many of topics in a variety of genres. She is best known for the popular Guardians of Ga'hoole series of fantasy novels.

Born June 24, 1944 in Indianapolis, Ind., Lasky was an enthusiastic storyteller as a child, and her mother began encouraging her to write when she was 10 years old. She went to an all-girls private school in Indiana before going to Michigan State University to study English. After graduating in 1966, Lasky worked as a teacher while honing her skills as a writer.

In 1975, Lasky published the first of many children's books, *Agatha's Alphabet*. A year later, she published *I Have Four Names for My Grandfather* (1976). This was the first of Lasky's many collaborations with her husband, the photographer Christopher G. Knight. *The Weaver's Gift*

(1981) was the first of Lasky's books to receive a major award. Produced with her husband, the book is a photo essay documenting a weaver named Carolyn Frye who produces wool products from sheep she raises herself. The book won the Boston Globe/Horn Book Award in 1981.

Lasky's 1981 young adult novel *The Night Journey* is highly regarded for its engagement with Jewish history. The novel is based on the true story of a nine-year-old Jewish girl's efforts to help her family escape religious persecution in Russia. The novel won the National Jewish Book Award for children's literature in 1982. Lasky revisited the subject of *The Night Journey* with her 2005 novel *Broken Song.*

Between 2003 and 2010, Lasky published sixteen books in the Guardians of Ga'hoole series. Lasky lived near Harvard University in Cambridge, Mass., while writing the novels, and she frequently consulted with scientists in the ornithology department for information on owls for the books. The first three novels of the series were adapted for the 2010 animated film *Legend of the Guardians: The Owls of Ga'hoole.*

# DENNIS LEHANE

(b. 1965– )

Dennis Lehane is an American author who is best known for his suspenseful mystery novels, including *Mystic River* (2001; film 2010). He has also written television scripts, screenplays for film, and a collection of short stories, *Coronado* (2006), which includes a two-act play *Until Gwen*.

Born Aug. 4, 1965, Lehane was born and raised in the Dorchester neighborhood of Boston, Mass. He studied creative writing as an undergraduate at Eckerd College, and earned a master's in fine arts degree from Florida International University in 1993. Before becoming a writer, Lehane worked as a counselor for emotionally handicapped children, and as an English teacher at Florida International University.

Lehane published his first novel, *A Drink Before the War*, in 1995. The novel introduces Patrick Kenzie and Angela Gennaro, a pair of young, hard-edged private detectives in Boston. *A Drink Before the War* was well received and won the Shamus Award for Best First Private Investigator Novel. Kenzie and Gennaro

*Dennis Lehane.* **Boston Globe/Getty Images**

reappear as the protagonists of Lehane's subsequent novels *Darkness, Take My Hand* (1996), *Sacred* (1997), *Gone, Baby, Gone* (1998), *Prayers for Rain* (1999), and *Moonlight Mile* (2010).

Three of Lehane's novels, *Mystic River, Gone, Baby, Gone* (film 2007), and *Shutter Island* (2003; film 2010), have been made into highly acclaimed films. *Mystic River* is an unconventional mystery noir set in a working class neighborhood of Boston about three former childhood friends, Dave Boyle, Jimmy Marcus, and Sean Devine, who are brought together as adults when Marcus's daughter is found murdered. The film adaptation of *Mystic River*, directed by Clint Eastwood and starring Sean Penn, Kevin Bacon, and Tim Robbins, was nominated for six Academy Awards, including best picture. Lehane has also written a number of episodes for the HBO series *The Wire*.

# YANN MARTEL

(b. 1963– )

Yann Martel is a Canadian author best known for his Booker Prize–winning novel, *Life of Pi* (2001).

Martel was born June 25, 1963, in Salamanca, Spain. Martel's parents worked for the Canadian Foreign Service, and the family moved frequently. Martel grew up in Costa Rica, France, Spain, Mexico, and Canada. He went to Trent University in Peterborough, Ont., where he earned an honours B.A. in philosophy in 1985. Martel has since lived in Iran, Turkey, India, Montreal, and Saskatoon, Can. Although Martel began writing soon after college, he worked several jobs before

*Yann Martel.* Keith Beaty/Toronto Star/Getty Images

turning to writing full-time when he was twenty-seven years old.

Martel published a short story, "The Facts Behind the Helsinki Roccamatios," in a literary magazine called the *Malahat Review* in 1990. The story won the Journey Prize for best Canadian short story, and was later included in Martel's *The Facts Behind the Helsinki Roccamatios and Other Stories* (1993). Martel published his first novel, *Self,* in 1996. The imaginative story unfolds as an autobiography of a widely traveled, gender-shifting young person's life leading up to a devastating traumatic event. Although *Self* was well reviewed by critics, it was not until the publication of his critically acclaimed 2001 novel *Life of Pi* that Martel achieved far-reaching success. The novel tells the fantastic story of Pi Patel, the son of Indian zookeepers whose family decides to immigrate to Canada with a ship full of animals. When the ship is wrecked during the voyage, Pi is stranded aboard a lifeboat with several animals, including a Bengal tiger. The novel won the prestigious Man Booker Prize in 2002, and the 2012 film adaptation of the novel was nominated for numerous Academy Awards. Martel has since published another collection of short stories entitled *We Ate the Children Last* (2004) and the novel *Beatrice and Virgil* (2010).

# CORMAC MCCARTHY

(b. 1933– )

Often compared to such classic American authors as William Faulkner and Herman Melville, U.S. novelist Cormac McCarthy, with his gift for metaphor and his unerring ear for local dialect, has written novels about youth, violence, and the changing American landscape.

Charles Joseph (Cormac) McCarthy was born on July 20, 1933, in Providence, R.I. When he was four years old, his father joined the legal staff of the Tennessee Valley Authority and moved the family of six children to Knoxville, Tenn. After graduating from the local Catholic high school, Cormac enrolled at the Knoxville campus of the University of Tennessee. In 1953, he abruptly left the university to join the U.S. Air Force.

After being discharged from service in 1956, McCarthy resumed his studies at the university the following year. His fiction, first published in the school's literary magazine, began to attract critical attention, and he won the Ingram Merrill Award for creative writing in 1959 and 1960. McCarthy left college without finishing his degree to pursue a writing career. With his wife, fellow student Lee Holleman, and their son, Cullen, McCarthy moved to Chicago, where he worked as an auto mechanic while writing his first novel. The McCarthys moved back to Tennessee several years later, and the marriage ended shortly thereafter.

McCarthy's first four novels, which focused on people and events in Tennessee and Appalachia, established him in literary circles as a regional writer of the Appalachian South. *The Orchard Keeper* (1965), winner of the William Faulkner award, was the story of a young boy coming of age in a small community in rural Tennessee.

In 1965, McCarthy received a traveling fellowship from the American Academy of Arts and Letters. En route to Ireland, the land of his ancestors, he met a young

Englishwoman named Anne DeLisle. They were married in England in 1966, and the couple toured Europe before settling on Ibiza, a small island off the coast of Spain, where McCarthy finished writing his second novel, *Outer Dark*, which was published the following year. McCarthy and his second wife returned to Tennessee in 1967.

His third novel, *Child of God* (1973), was a chilling tale inspired by a historical murder case in Tennessee. McCarthy then wrote a screenplay for the Public Broadcasting System called *The Gardener's Son* (1976), which was a drama, based on historical events, of the fatefully tangled lives of two families in post–Civil War South Carolina.

McCarthy and his second wife separated in 1976. Shortly after that, McCarthy moved to El Paso, Tex., where he finished his fourth novel, *Suttree* (1979). A book 20 years in the making, it was an unwavering portrait of one man in all his personal triumphs and failings, who ekes out a living from a river that symbolizes the elemental forces of life, nature, and death. McCarthy received a fellowship from the MacArthur Foundation in

1981, and he lived on the proceeds while researching and writing his next novel, a book that would mark the shift in his literary focus from the American rural South to the American Southwest.

Many critics regarded *Blood Meridian* (1985) as McCarthy's finest work to date. It was a new breed of the Western novel that, unlike its predecessors, exhibited no sentimentality and no moral judgment of characters or events. Set in Texas and Mexico during the 1840s, the story, based on actual historical figures and events, recounted the nightmarish adventures of a young man from Tennessee who travels West and eventually joins a band of lawless scalp hunters.

In McCarthy's famed Border Trilogy, in which he rewrote and challenged the myths of the American wild West, the border between Mexico and the United States was used as a metaphor for the borderland between progress and dehumanization and between history and myth. The first volume of the trilogy, *All the Pretty Horses* (1992), not only garnered many excellent reviews, but, unlike McCarthy's previous novels, also enjoyed commercial success. It became a *New York Times* best seller and the winner of the 1992 National Book Award and the National Book Critics Circle Award. The second volume of the trilogy, *The Crossing* (1994), enjoyed even more commercial success than the first. These two volumes chronicled the respective coming-of-age stories of two boys who, as they journey between Texas and Mexico, experience the evils of humanity and painfully shed the innocence of childhood. The long awaited third volume, *Cities of the Plain* (1998), brought together the heroes of the first two volumes and recapitulated the themes of loss and exile.

# TERRY MCMILLAN

(b. 1951– )

Terry McMillan is an African American author, born in Port Huron, Mich., on Oct. 18, 1951. Her novels have reached a wide audience in the United States and have been praised for their story lines and characters that

reflect with energy and fervour the lives of contemporary black Americans.

McMillan's father was a blue-collar worker and her mother was a factory worker. They were divorced in 1964 and her mother supported Terry and her four brothers and sisters. The Bible was the only book in their house, but Terry worked at a local library while she was in high school and read James Baldwin and many other authors. She moved to Los Angeles and received a B.A. from the University of California at Berkeley.

McMillan moved to New York after graduation and entered a film program at Columbia University, which she left to pursue her writing. She won an American Book Award in 1987 for *Mama*, her first novel. Her second novel, *Disappearing Acts* (1989), was followed by an anthology of contemporary black fiction edited by McMillan, called *Breaking Ice* (1990). McMillan also developed a film adaptation of *Disappearing Acts*. Her third novel, *Waiting to Exhale* (1992), became a best seller in its first week in print. It told the story of four women friends and concerned the complex relationships of women and men. The novel brought a remarkable $2.64 million for paperback rights, and its success heightened the awareness of publishers and booksellers to a growing audience of middle-class African American readers. The book's wild popularity helped the author secure a $6 million publishing contract for her fourth novel, *How Stella Got Her Groove Back* (1996; film 1998), about a wealthy black woman of middle age who falls in love with a young cook while vacationing in Jamaica. McMillan's later novels include *A Day Late and a Dollar Short* (2001), *The Interruption of Everything* (2005), and *Getting to Happy* (2010), a sequel to *Waiting to Exhale*. She also wrote the nonfiction work *It's OK If You're Clueless: And 25 More Tips for the College Bound* (2006).

McMillan won a National Endowment for the Arts Fellowship in literature 1988 and a fellowship to the Yaddo artist colony. She taught creative writing and contemporary literature at the University of Wyoming and the University of Arizona at Tucson. She also gave dramatic readings from her works and reviewed books for the the *New York Times Book Review*, the *Atlanta Constitution*, and the *Philadelphia Inquirer*. In 1993 she won an NAACP Image Award in the literary category for *Waiting to Exhale*.

# ALAN MOORE

(b. 1953– )

Alan Moore is a British writer whose works—such as *V for Vendetta* and *Watchmen*—are some of the most influential books in the history of graphic narrative. His works have pushed the bounds of what is possible in comic books and graphic novels.

Alan Moore was born Nov. 18, 1953, in Northampton, Eng. He began working as a writer and artist for independent magazines in the early 1970s. He achieved mainstream success with the stories he wrote for *Doctor Who Weekly* and the science-fiction anthology series *2000 AD*. However, the full extent of his talents first became apparent in 1982, when he reinterpreted the classic British hero

Marvelman (called Miracleman in the United States) for the magazine *Warrior*. Moore rewrote Marvelman as a middle-aged reporter who had forgotten his role as the world's most important superhero. The stories explore how a person with superhuman powers would interact with human society.

Moore's next project, *V for Vendetta* (1982–86), imagines a world in which the ruling political party has almost total power. The story's masked hero is an intellectual terrorist named Guy Fawkes who works to overthrow the totalitarian regime. In 1983, DC Comics hired Moore to write *Swamp Thing*, a straightforward monster comic, which Moore used to explore serious themes of life and death. Moore's success with *Swamp Thing* led to *Watchmen*, a work that helped define the term *graphic novel* for many readers. Its mature story line and morally complex characters are unlike anything that had previously appeared in the superhero genre.

Moore's later works continue the tradition of taking on profound themes in comics. The Image Comics title *Supreme* examines the psychology of the superhero, and *Promethea* reimagines the character Wonder Woman as a way to explore Moore's beliefs about the Kabbala, a Jewish mystical tradition. *Promethea* was published by America's Best Comics, the imprint Moore started in 1999.

Although many of Moore's works have been made into movies, he has not been happy with them. *From Hell* (originally published from 1991–96), a complicated series that comments on the decline of the British Empire through the story of the Jack the Ripper killings, was turned into a straightforward action film with an unconvincing happy ending in 2001. *The League of Extraordinary Gentlemen* (first published in 1999) smartly reimagines famous characters from Victorian-era literature as British secret agents, but lost its literary flair when it appeared on film in 2003. Furthermore, the film added new characters—including a crime-fighting Tom Sawyer—to appeal to American audiences. Disappointed by his previous experiences with Hollywood, Moore dissociated himself from the film versions of *V for Vendetta* (2006) and *Watchmen* (2009), and his name did not appear in the credits. Moore was convinced that his ideas were best realized on the printed page.

# TONI MORRISON

(b. 1931– )

U.S. author Toni Morrison is noted for her examination of the African American experience (particularly the female experience) within the black community. Her use of fantasy, her intricate poetic style, and her rich interweaving of the mythic have given her stories great strength and texture. In 1993 she won the Nobel Prize for Literature.

Morrison was born Chloe Anthony Wofford on Feb. 18, 1931, in Lorain, Ohio. She grew up in a poor family but graduated from Howard University in Washington, D.C., in 1953 and received a master's degree in English from Cornell University in Ithaca, N.Y., in 1955. After several years as an English instructor, Morrison became an editor and wrote in her spare time.

127

Morrison's first novel, *The Bluest Eye* (1970), was a criticism of middle-class black life and of human intolerance. With the 1977 publication of *Song of Solomon*, which is told by a male narrator in search of his identity, Morrison received popular as well as critical acclaim. *Tar Baby* (1981), set on a Caribbean island, explores conflicts of race, class, and sex. *Beloved* won the 1988 Pulitzer Prize for Fiction. It is based on the true story of a runaway slave who, at the point of recapture, kills her infant daughter in order to spare her a life of slavery. Morrison's later works include *A Mercy* (2008), which deals with slavery in 17th-century America, and *Home* (2012), about a traumatized Korean War veteran who encounters racism after returning home and later overcomes apathy to rescue his sister.

Besides her novels, Morrison published a work of criticism, *Playing in the Dark: Whiteness and the Literary Imagination*, in 1992. Many of her essays and speeches were collected in *What Moves at the Margin: Selected Nonfiction* (edited by Carolyn C. Denard), published in 2008. In addition, Morrison released several children's books, including *Who's Got Game?: The Ant or the Grasshopper?* and *Who's Got Game?: The Lion or the Mouse?*, both written with her son and published in 2003. *Remember* (2004), also aimed at children, uses archival photographs to

*U.S. Pres. Barack Obama presenting the Presidential Medal of Freedom to Toni Morrison during a ceremony at the White House, May 29, 2012. The award is the highest honor a civilian can receive from the United States government.* Mandel Ngan/AFP/Getty Images

chronicle the hardships of black students during the integration of the U.S. public school system. Morrison also wrote the libretto for *Margaret Garner* (2005), an opera about the same story that inspired *Beloved*.

In 2010 Morrison was made an officer of the French Legion of Honour. Two years later she was awarded the U.S. Presidential Medal of Freedom.

# ALICE MUNRO

(b. 1931– )

Canadian short-story writer Alice Munro is known for her intense narrative style and imagery.

Alice Anne Laidlaw was born in Wingham, Ont., on July 10, 1931. She began writing stories at age 15. She attended the University of Western Ontario, where she later became writer in residence.

Her first collection of stories, *Dance of the Happy Shades* (1968), won the Governor General's Literary Award for Fiction. Her

*Who Do You Think You Are?* (1978) and *The Progress of Love* (1986) also won that award. Her second collection—*The Lives of Girls and Women* (1971), a group of coming-of-age stories—was followed by *Something I've Been Meaning to Tell You* (1974), *The Moons of Jupiter* (1982), *Friend of My Youth* (1986), *A Wilderness Station* (1994), and *The Love of a Good Woman* (1998). In 1977 Munro became the first Canadian to win the Canada-Australia Literary Prize. She was also the first Canadian nominated for the *Irish Times*–Aer Lingus Fiction Prize, with *Friend of My Youth* (1990).

Her book *Open Secrets* (1994) contains stories that range in setting from the hills of southern Ontario to the mountains of Albania. In *Runaway* (2004) Munro explores the depths of ordinary lives, and *The View from Castle Rock* (2007) combines history, family memoir, and fiction. In 2009 Munro won the Man Booker International Prize; that same year she published the short-story collection *Too Much Happiness*. Like much of her work, the stories in *Dear Life* (2012) were characterized by explorations of sex, love, and death. Four of the stories in the collection were framed as fictionalized autobiography meant to reflect the aging Munro's feelings about her life.

Munro's short story about the domestic hardships of Alzheimer's disease, "The Bear Came over the Mountain" (2001), was made into the critically acclaimed film *Away from Her* (2006). Munro, who in June of 2013 accepted a literary prize for *Dear Life*, later that year was awarded the Nobel Prize in Literature as "master of the contemporary short story."

# PHYLLIS REYNOLDS NAYLOR

(b. 1933– )

U.S. writer Phyllis Reynolds Naylor, the author of more than 70 books for children and adults, has made a name for herself in a variety of genres.

Naylor was born on Jan. 4, 1933, in Anderson, Ind. She began writing stories in grade school and was published in a church paper as a teenager. In 1963, she received a bachelor's degree in psychology from

American University but decided to forgo graduate school to devote herself to writing full-time. She began publishing collections of short stories for children and young adults in 1965, and her first children's novel, *What the Gulls Were Singing*, appeared in 1967.

Naylor received numerous awards for her work, most notably the 1991 Newbery Medal for *Shiloh*, a story about a boy who discovers the complexity of decision making while trying to save an abused dog. Her nonfiction book *How I Became a Writer* (1978) earned a Golden Kite Award from the Society of Children's Book Writers. She was honoured by the Child Study Association of America for her fictional *Wrestle the Mountain* (1971), *How Lazy Can You Get?* (1979), and *The Agony of Alice* (1985), and the Mystery Writers of America presented her with the Edgar Allan Poe Award for *Night Cry* (1984).

Naylor wrote several series of novels. The 1970s Witch trilogy (*Witch's Sister* [1975], *Witch Water* [1977], and *The Witch Herself* [1978]) proved so successful that she wrote more sequels during the 1990s. She launched the York collection, about a teenage time-traveler seeking a cure for Huntington's disease, with *Shadows on the*

*Wall* (1980), and she began the Bessledorf series of humorous mysteries with *The Mad Gasser of Bessledorf Street* (1983).

Among Naylor's other publications were the children's comedy *Beetles, Lightly Toasted* (1987), the realistic adolescent novels *A String of Chances* (1982) and *The Year of the Gopher* (1987), and the adult novel *Revelations* (1979). Recollections of her first husband's mental illness formed the adult nonfiction book *Crazy Love: An Autobiographical Account of Marriage and Madness* (1977). The subject also inspired the young adult novel *The Keeper* (1986), later shown on television as the ABC Afterschool Special *My Dad Can't Be Crazy, Can He?* (1989). She also wrote advice books about relationships.

# CHRISTOPHER NOLAN

(b. 1965–d. 2009)

Unable to move or speak from birth, Irish author Christopher Nolan nevertheless won recognition as a gifted writer at an early age. At 21 he published *Under the Eye of the Clock*, an autobiographical novel that won Great Britain's prestigious Whitbread Prize in 1987. His lyrical and adventurous poetry and prose were likened to the work of fellow Irish writers William Butler Yeats, Samuel Beckett, and James Joyce.

Nolan was born on Sept. 6, 1965, in Mullingar, Ire. At birth he suffered severe brain damage that left him speechless and paralyzed with a condition now known as dystomia. During childhood he began taking a drug that permitted him slight movement. Nolan indicated to his family that he wanted to write, but he was unable to grasp a pencil. At the suggestion of a physical therapist, Nolan's family made him a "unicorn stick," which they strapped to his forehead. Using the stick, Nolan was able to peck out letters on a keyboard, and he began writing. In 1981 a collection of his plays, stories, poems, and autobiographical material was published as *Dam-Burst of Dreams*.

Nolan published *Under the Eye of the Clock* in 1987. Written in the third person, the book tells the story of Joseph Meehan, whose life closely resembles Nolan's. His vivid memoir is never bitter, though it recounts some of the more traumatic moments he experienced in the world of "normal children." Nolan was praised for his fine ability to look at himself from a distance. In 1999 he published his novel *The Banyan Tree*, which took him 12 years to complete. A departure from his previous autobiographical work, the novel chronicles the life of Minnie O'Brien, a rural Irish woman born at the beginning of the 20th century. As in his previous work, Nolan's mesmerizing and melodious prose displayed his linguistic agility and his genius for coining new words and innovative turns of phrase. He died Feb. 20, 2009, in Dublin, Ireland.

# JOYCE CAROL OATES

(b. 1938– )

An American author born on June 16, 1938, in Lockport, N.Y., Oates is known as a prolific writer of poems, essays, plays, novels, and short stories. She was an instructor of English at the University of Detroit from 1961 to 1967 and a member of

*Joyce Carol Oates.* Francois Durand/Getty Images

the English department at the University of Windsor in Canada from 1967 to 1978. She became writer-in-residence at Princeton University in 1978. Oates won many honours for her work, including the O. Henry Prize in 1967 for her short story "In the Region of Ice" and the National Book Award in 1970 for her novel *them*. Her other novels include *Wonderland* (1972), *Do With Me What You Will* (1973), *The Assassins* (1975), *Bellefleur* (1980), *Bloodsmoor Romance* (1983), *Black Water* (1992), *Foxfire: Confessions of a Girl Gang* (1993), *Zombie* (1995), *We Were the Mulvaneys* (1996), *Broke Heart Blues* (1999), *The Falls* (2004), *My Sister, My Love: The Intimate Story of Skyler Rampike* (2008), *Mudwoman* (2012), and *Daddy Love* (2013). Her forays into young adult fiction include *Big Mouth & Ugly Girl* (2002) and *Two or Three Things I Forgot to Tell You* (2012).

Oates has also written mysteries (under the pseudonyms Rosamond Smith and Lauren Kelly), plays, essays, poetry, and literary criticism. Essays, reviews, and other prose pieces are included in *Where I've Been, and Where I'm Going* (1999) and *In Rough Country* (2010). In 2011 Oates published the memoir *A Widow's Story*, in which she mourns her husband's death.

# TIM O'BRIEN

(b. 1946– )

Tim O'Brien is an American novelist noted for his writings about American soldiers in the Vietnam War.

O'Brien was born Oct. 1, 1946, in Austin, Minn. After studying political science at Macalester College, St. Paul, Minn., (B.A., 1968), O'Brien fought in Vietnam. When he returned to the United States, he studied intermittently at Harvard University and worked for the *Washington Post* (1971–74) as an intern and reporter. He collected his newspaper and magazine articles about his war experiences in his first book, *If I Die in a Combat Zone, Box Me Up and Ship Me Home* (1973). By turns meditative and brutally realistic, it was praised for its honest portrayal of a soldier's emotions.

The Vietnam War is present in many of O'Brien's novels. One of the two main characters in *Northern Lights* (1975) is a wounded war hero. Set in an isolated, snow-covered part of Minnesota during a disastrous cross-country ski trip, the novel is an examination of courage. *Going After Cacciato* (1978), which won a National Book Award, follows both a soldier who abandons his platoon in Vietnam to try to walk to Paris and a fellow infantryman who escapes the war's horrors by inventing elaborate fantasies about his journey. *In The Things They Carried* (1990), a fictional narrator named Tim O'Brien begins his memoir with a description of the items that the members of his platoon took to war, which range from physical objects, such as weapons and love letters, to emotions of terror and homesickness. While a man's lifelong fear of dying from a nuclear bombing is the subject of *The Nuclear Age* (1981), *In the Lake of the Woods* (1994) returns to the subject of the experiences and effects of the Vietnam War. O'Brien's writing took a new turn with the publication of *Tomcat in Love* (1999), a nuanced comic novel about the search for love, and *July, July* (2002), whose disillusioned characters gather for a college class reunion.

# AMOS OZ

(b. 1939– )

A mos Oz is an Israeli author whose novels, short stories, and nonfiction

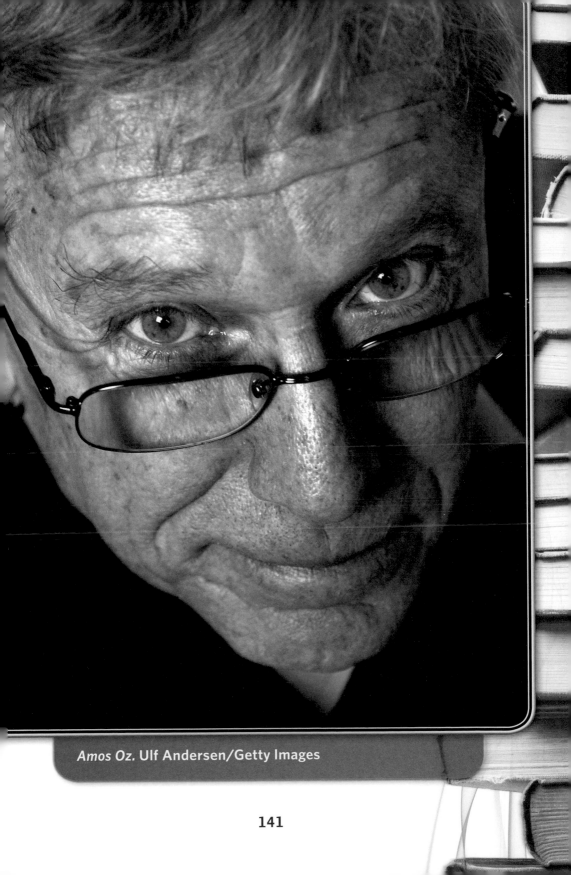

*Amos Oz.* Ulf Andersen/Getty Images

works often reflect the strains between secular and religious Jews and between Jews and their Arab neighbors. Despite his opinions about the mistakes his country has made, Oz is one of Israel's most popular writers. He has written more than a dozen novels and over 400 essays and articles and has received many accolades both at home and abroad for his writing, including the German Publishers International Peace Prize in 1992.

Oz was born Amos Klausner on May 4, 1939, in Jerusalem. Amos grew up during a time of rapid change in Israel. Palestine was under British rule, and many Jews went there to escape the Nazis in the late 1930s and early 1940s. When the British left the region in 1948, Amos and his schoolmates helped prepare for Israel's War of Independence by filling sandbags.

Soon after his mother committed suicide in 1952, Amos joined a settlement called Kibbutz Hulda where he learned the principles of communal life. He also changed his name to the Hebrew word *oz*, which means "strength." Oz was drafted into the Israeli Army in 1957. After the required three years of army service, he went to Hebrew University in Jerusalem, where he received a bachelor's degree in literature and philosophy in 1963.

Oz published his first book, *Where the Jackals Howl*, in 1965. The collection of stories reflects communal life on a kibbutz as well as a longing for urban life. His first novel, *Elsewhere, Perhaps* (1966), describes the generation of refugees from Russia and Germany that settled many kibbutzim. Oz's 1968 novel, *My Michael*, was his first best seller. Set in Jerusalem in the 1950s, the novel uses the story of a failing marriage as an allegory for Israeli society. By the early 1970s, Oz had earned an international reputation. Among his many other works of fiction are *Soumchi* (1978), a children's story about a boy's life in Jerusalem after World War II that won Germany's Luchs Prize for children's books in 1993, and *Fima* (1991), which was a *New York Times* notable book of the year.

Oz joined the Israeli peace movement in the early 1970s. He was a founding member of Peace Now, and he led the organization beginning in 1977. He argued that Israel could be a truly pluralistic society only if it enabled the Palestinians to create their own state. In the early 1980s,

Oz traveled through Israel and interviewed Jews and Arabs of all backgrounds. The resulting book, *In the Land of Israel* (1983), is an often unsettling and painfully honest work about the state of the country. His other nonfiction works include the anthology *Different People* (1974) and *Israel, Palestine, and Peace* (1994).

In addition to his writing and activism, Oz has been a dedicated teacher. He taught literature and philosophy at Hulda High School and Givat Brenner Regional High School from 1963 to 1986. He has worked as a writer in residence and taught literature at Colorado College, the University of California at Berkeley, Boston University, and Hebrew University. Oz became a professor of Hebrew literature at Ben Gurion University in 1987 and was appointed to the Agnon Chair in Modern Hebrew in 1990.

# ANN PATCHETT

(b. 1963– )

Anne Patchett is an American author whose novels have often portrayed the intersecting lives of characters from disparate backgrounds.

Born Dec. 2, 1963, in Los Angeles, Calif., when Patchett was six years old her family moved to Nashville, Tenn., where she grew up and where she made her home. She obtained a B.A. degree (1984) from Sarah Lawrence College, Bronxville, N.Y., and an M.F.A. (1987) from the University of Iowa. Her first work of fiction was published while she was an undergraduate. Patchett later held appointments at colleges and universities, including the position of Tennessee Williams Fellow in Creative Writing at the University of the South in Sewanee, Tenn., in 1997. From the beginning of her career, she won numerous awards for her writing, and in 1994 she received a Guggenheim Fellowship.

Though she was widely published as a short-story writer and essayist, Patchett became best known for her novels. Her first novel, *The Patron Saint of Liars* (1992), tells the story of a young pregnant woman who leaves the husband she does not love to travel to a home for unwed mothers. There, as her feelings change and she creates a new family, so do her plans for the future. The novel was adapted as a television movie in 1997. In *Taft* (1994) the black manager of a blues bar who is mourning the loss of his son finds a new family when he hires a young white woman, Fay Taft, and becomes involved in the problems of her brother, Carl. Patchett also wrote a screen adaptation of the novel. *The Magician's Assistant* (1997) relates the discoveries of the widow of a homosexual magician named Parsifal. The woman, who also had been her husband's assistant, visits the family he had never told her of and learns about his past.

With her fourth novel, *Bel Canto*, Patchett established her prominence among contemporary writers. The novel, set somewhere in South America, explores relationships between terrorists and hostages who, shut off from the rest of the world, find unexpected bonds. One of the hostages is a renowned operatic diva, and music becomes the medium by which the characters in the novel communicate. The novel received the PEN/Faulkner Award and the Orange Prize for Fiction and was a finalist for the National Book Critics Circle Award.

In 2005 Patchett published her first full-length volume of nonfiction writing, *Truth and Beauty*, a memoir recounting her friendship with the writer Lucy Grealy, who died of a drug overdose in 2002. Patchett returned to fiction with her next book, *Run* (2007), which explores the relationship between an ambitious father and his two sons. Issues of medical ethics and mortality are the focus of *State of Wonder* (2011), in which a pharmaceutical researcher travels to the Amazon rain forest to investigate both the death of a colleague and a scientist's work on an infertility drug.

# CHAIM POTOK

(b. 1929–d. 2002)

C haim Potok was an American rabbi and author whose novels introduced the spiritual and cultural life of Orthodox Jews to American fiction.

Herman Harold Potok was born Feb. 17, 1929 in New York City. The son of Polish immigrants, Potok was reared in an Orthodox home and attended religious schools. As a young man, he was drawn to the less restrictive Conservative branch of Judaism. After graduation from Yeshiva University in 1950 and the Jewish Theological Seminary of America in 1954 (both in New York City), he was ordained a Conservative rabbi. He taught at Jewish institutions of higher learning until he was named managing editor of the magazine *Conservative Judaism* in 1964. He later attended the University of Pennsylvania and in 1965 became editor in chief of the Jewish Publication Society of America, a post he held until 1974, when he became special-projects editor. Throughout his publishing career Potok wrote scholarly and popular articles and reviews.

Potok's first novel was *The Chosen* (1967; film 1981). It was the first book from a major publisher to portray Orthodox Judaism in the United States. The author established his reputation with this story of a Hasidic rabbi's son and the son's friend, whose humane Orthodox father encourages him to study non-religious subjects. The popular book was praised for its vivid rendering of the closed Hasidic community; some thought it an allegory of the survival of Judaism. *The Promise* (1969) followed the same characters to young adulthood. Potok again turned to the Hasidim in *My Name Is Asher Lev* (1972; play 2012), which tells of a young artist in conflict with the traditions of his family and community.

Potok's next four novels, the autobiographical *In the Beginning* (1975), *The Book of Lights* (1981), *Davita's Harp* (1985), and *The Gift of Asher Lev* (1990), also examine the conflict between religious and secular interests. *I Am the Clay* appeared in 1992, the illustrated *The Tree of Here* in 1993, *The Sky of Now* in 1995, and *Old Men at Midnight*, three connected novellas, in 2001. Notable among Potok's nonfiction writings are *Wanderings: Chaim Potok's History of the Jews* (1978), in which the author combines impressive scholarship with dramatic narrative, and *The Gates of November* (1996), a chronicle of a Soviet Jewish family and the rise and fall of the Soviet Union. Potok died July 23, 2002, in Merion, Pa.

# HENRY ROTH

(b. 1906–d. 1995)

U.S. author Henry Roth is best known for two things: he produced a literary masterpiece when he was barely 28 years old, and then he underwent one of the most profound and prolonged cases of writer's block ever. Roth's first novel appeared in 1934; his second was published 60 years later. During the six decades following the publication of *Call It Sleep*, Roth among other things worked as a toolmaker, woodsman, schoolteacher, attendant in a mental hospital, and water-fowl farmer. Periodically and with great frustration he tried to write. He produced a few short stories while unsuccessfully attempting to regain the brilliance that marked his first effort.

Perhaps more than any other American author, Roth blended fiction and auto-biography into a confessional style. The troubling family dynamics so powerfully portrayed in his writing existed to a sig-nificant extent within Roth's own family. Like David Schearl, the young boy in *Call It Sleep*, Henry Roth was born in the Austro-Hungarian province of Galicia on Feb. 8, 1906, and arrived at Ellis Island in New York in 1909 before beginning life in America on New York City's Lower East Side. Roth's family moved to what was then the Italian and Irish neighbor-hood of Harlem when he was eight, at which point he began to lose his Jewish identity, a theme that would recur in his writing. Roth lived with his family until 1927, when as a junior at City College of New York he came under the personal and professional influence of professor and poet Eda Lou Walton, with whose encouragement *Call It Sleep* was written and to whom the novel is dedicated.

In 1938, at the artists' colony Yaddo in upstate New York, Roth met and within a year married the pianist and composer Muriel Parker. By the time Roth met Parker he was deeply involved in the Communist movement within the United States, an experience he eventually found extremely disillusioning. After the 1967 Six-Day War in Israel, Roth began a reassessment of his Jewishness that began with a repudiation of Communism, led to a commitment to Israel, and concluded with an acceptance of himself as a Jew.

Ultimately Roth was able to again use his life as inspiration, overcoming his block and producing in 1994 his second, multi-volume novel, collectively titled *Mercy of a*

*Rude Stream.* Both novels provide an evocative retrospective of American culture from the points of view of two very similar Jewish boys. Truth is a redemptive theme in both of these novels, each of which portrays the futile quest of a gifted child (and, in later volumes of *Mercy*, the man grown from the child) to find a place in a frightening and confusing world.

In 1994, Roth received two honorary doctorates, one from the University of New Mexico and one from the Hebrew Theological Institute in Cincinnati, Ohio. Roth died on Oct. 13, 1995, in Albuquerque, N.M., where he had lived for many years.

# ISAAC BASHEVIS SINGER

(b. 1904–d. 1991)

Writing in the language of his ancestors, Isaac Bashevis Singer drew a large audience to his depictions of Jewish life in Eastern Europe in the 19th and

20th centuries. The author once wrote, "In a figurative way, Yiddish is the wise and humble language of us all, the idiom of the frightened and hopeful humanity." Although Singer moved to the United States in 1935 and became a naturalized citizen in 1943, he continued to write all of his works in Yiddish, and he supervised their translation into many other languages. From his first years in the United States, when he worked as a journalist for the *Jewish Daily Forward*, Singer tried to be optimistic about the future of the Yiddish language.

Singer was born on July 14, 1904, in Radzymin, Pol., into a family of Hasidic rabbis. He studied at a rabbinical seminary near his home but knew early on that he wanted to be a writer. For Singer literature was a means of telling stories, and all of his writings reflect the long tradition of storytelling. Most of his works take place in the *shtetl*, or small Jewish village, and define the world of European Jews before World War II. His characters are often preoccupied with problems of faith and sin and the relationship between human beings and God. His stories are often filled with magical, mystical moments, and ghosts and spirits are as central to the plots as the living characters.

Singer died in a nursing home in Florida on July 24, 1991. In his long career Singer won many prizes, including the 1978 Nobel Prize for Literature, the Newbery Book Award, and the National Book Award. His works include such novels as *The Family Moskat*, published in 1950, *The Magician of Lublin* (1960), *The Estate* (1969), *Enemies, a Love Story* (1972), and *Shosha* (1978); short-story collections such as *Gimpel the Fool* (1957), *The Spinoza of Market Street* (1961), *The Seance* (1968), and *A Crown of Feathers* (1973); many works for children, including *Zlateh the Goat* (1966), *Schlemiel Went to Warsaw, and Other Stories* (1968), and *A Tale of Three Wishes* (1975); and autobiographical writings that include *In My Father's Court* (1966) and *A Young Man in Search of Love* (1978).

Several films have been adapted from Singer's works, including *The Magician of Lublin* (1979), based on his novel of the same name, and *Yentl* (1983), based on his story "Yentl" in *Mayses fun hintern oyvn* (1971; "Stories from Behind the Stove").

# ZADIE SMITH

(b. 1975– )

Zadie Smith is a British author who became an overnight sensation when her first novel *White Teeth* was published in 2000. The novel explores race, religion, and cultural identity through the humorous exploits of an extensive cast of vibrantly drawn characters. *White Teeth* introduces the major themes that Smith returns to repeatedly throughout her career.

Sadie Smith was born in the Willesden area of London, Eng., on Oct. 25, 1975. She is the daughter of a Jamaican mother and an English father. She changed her first name to Zadie when she was 14 years old. Smith was just 21 years old when she submitted 80 pages of *White Teeth* to a literary agent. This small sample, which eventually became a novel of over 400 pages, caused a bidding war for the publication rights. The finished novel was a best seller. *White Teeth* won numerous awards, including the Whitbread First Novel Award (2000), and was a finalist for the National Book Critics Circle Award and the Orange Prize for Fiction.

Although it did not earn the high praise of *White Teeth*, Smith's second novel, *The Autograph Man* (2002), received mostly positive reviews from critics. *The Autograph Man* addresses human beings' obsession with celebrity and pop culture. Her next novel, *On Beauty* (2005), reinforced Smith's reputation as one of the top British novelists of her generation. Closely modeled on E.M. Forster's 1910 novel *Howards End, On Beauty* satirizes the "culture wars" and deals with race and ethnicity in a fictional American town. It was a finalist for the Man Booker Prize and won the 2006 Orange Prize for Fiction.

In *NW* (2012), Smith explores the long-term effects that place and socioeconomic conditions of people's upbringing have on their lives through the stories of four people who grew up in the same section of northwest London. *NW* is more experimental and less humorous than Smith's previous novels and it was received poorly by critics. Smith has also edited and contributed to the short-story collection *The*

*Zadie Smith winning the 2006 Orange Prize for Fiction, London, Eng.* Tomos Brangwyn/WireImage/Getty Images

*Book of Other People* (2007) and published
a collection of essays, *Changing My Mind*
(2009). She teaches in the creative writing
program at New York University.

# NICHOLAS SPARKS

(b. 1965– )

Nicholas Sparks is an American author
known for his romance novels, all of
which have been *New York Times* best sellers.
His books have been translated into more
than 50 languages, and eight of his novels
have been adapted for film.

Sparks was born in Omaha, Neb., on
New Year's Eve in 1965. In addition to being
valedictorian of his high school class, Sparks
was an impressive athlete. He received a
full athletic scholarship to run track at the
University of Notre Dame, where his team
set the record for the 4 x 800-metre relay.
He earned a bachelor's degree in business
finance in 1988.

Sparks began writing in college while
recovering from a track injury. After
writing an unpublished novel, Sparks
coauthored the motivational work

Nicholas Sparks arriving at the 2012 Los Angeles premiere of *The Lucky One* at Grauman's Chinese Theatre in Hollywood, Calif. Gregg DeGuire/FilmMagic/Getty Images

*Wokini: A Lakota Journey to Happiness and Self-Understanding* (1995) with the Native American Olympic gold medal winner Billy Mills. It was not until the publication of *The Notebook* in 1996, however, that Sparks achieved mainstream success. Written when Sparks was 28 years old, *The Notebook* is a sentimental love story set in the South about a young woman who is torn between the man her family wants her to marry and the man she loves. The novel was made into a 2004 film starring Ryan Gosling and Rachel McAdams. Sparks has since published 15 more novels, including *Message in a Bottle* (1998; film 1999), *A Walk to Remember* (1999; film 2002), *The Lucky One* (2008; film 2012), and *Safe Haven* (2010; film 2013). His 2003 novel, *The Guardian,* infuses his usual romance with the darker elements of a thriller. Written with his brother Micah, the memoir *Three Weeks With My Brother* (2004) documents the journey the two men took to various locations around the world in 2003.

In 2006, Sparks and his wife, Catherine, founded The Epiphany School for Global Studies in New Bern, North Carolina. The K–12 independent Christian school focuses on preparing its students for life in the international community. The Nicholas Sparks Foundation was established in 2011 to expand the Sparks family's educational philanthropy. Sparks is also a major financial supporter of the Master's of Fine Arts Program in Creative Writing at the University of Notre Dame.

# ART SPIEGELMAN

(b. 1948– )

Holocaust literature is an expansive, compelling genre that continues to grow and diversify as it struggles to convey events so horrible they are often difficult to accept. By contrast, comic books are rarely recognized for their literary competence or historical value. In his two volumes, *Maus I: A Survivor's Tale: My Father Bleeds History* and *Maus II: A Survivor's Tale: And Here My Troubles Began*, author and artist Art Spiegelman not only established the comic book as a mainstream art form but also produced a work that, in chronicling one man's Holocaust ordeal, deepens the reader's understanding of those events.

*Maus II*, published five years after its predecessor, concludes the powerful and true story of Spiegelman's parents—Vladek and Anja—both survivors of the Auschwitz death camp. Compelling in its ironic anthropomorphic animal depictions—the Jews are drawn as mice and the Nazis as cats—its historical veracity, and its personal accounts, the story is made more complex by its framework. Spiegelman portrays himself as Artie Spiegelman attempting to understand and reconstruct his parents' past while coping with his mother's suicide, his stingy, manipulative father, and his own sense of guilt.

The commercial and critical success of *Maus* earned Spiegelman a "Special Award" Pulitzer Prize in 1992 and a solo exhibit at New York City's Museum of Modern Art. In addition, *Maus II* became a *New York Times* best seller. Initially appearing on the fiction list, it was moved to nonfiction after Spiegelman appealed for the transfer on the basis of the book's carefully researched, factual scenes.

Born on Feb. 15, 1948, in Stockholm, Swe., Spiegelman immigrated to the United States with his family. He began selling cartoons and illustrations to

*Art Spiegelman posing before his artwork.* **Hermann J. Knippertz/dapd/AP Images**

the *Long Island* (N.Y.) *Post* at age 14. Spiegelman attended Harpur College (now the State University of New York at Binghamton) from 1965 to 1968 and worked as a designer, writer, and artist for Topps Chewing Gum, where he helped develop the satirical Garbage Pail Kids and Wacky Packages bubble-gum cards.

In 1980 he cofounded and coedited *Raw*, an underground comic and graphics journal. With his wife, Françoise Mouly, an artist and publisher, he sought to present graphic novels and "comix" (comics written for a mature audience, as distinguished from the mass-produced variety created for children and adolescents) to a wider public. Recognized as the leading avant-garde comix journal, *Raw* featured the work of European artists as well as previewing Spiegelman's own work. The success and acceptance of *Raw* and *Maus* resulted in a wider commercial audience for Spiegelman and work as a *New York Times* illustrator and *Playboy* cartoonist.

In 2000 Spiegelman and Mouly launched *Little Lit*, a comics anthology for children that collected work from comics creators Chris Ware, Neil Gaiman (also an established writer), and Daniel Clowes, children's authors Maurice Sendak and Lemony Snicket, and humorist David Sedaris, among others. Although Spiegelman achieved success with lighthearted fare for young readers—his *Open Me...I'm a Dog!* (1997) was well received—he was inspired by the events of Sept. 11, 2001, to return to the comix format. Stating that "disaster is my muse," Spiegelman published *In the Shadow of No Towers* (2004), a collection of broadsheet-sized meditations on mortality and the far-reaching consequences of that day. In 2008 he released *Breakdowns: Portrait of the Artist as a Young %@&\*!,* which repackaged his long out-of-print *Breakdowns* collection as part of a longer graphic memoir.

# REBECCA STEAD

(b. 1968– )

U.S. author Rebecca Stead stumbled into the world of children's literature and has been welcomed there ever since. A former lawyer and public defender, Stead's second young adult book won the Newbery Medal in 2010.

Stead was born in New York City on Jan. 16, 1968. As a child, she was constantly on the wait for her magical powers to manifest. When they failed to appear, Stead turned to books, where she found a different sort of magic that was more probable. In 1989 she graduated from Vassar College with a bachelor's degree, and in 1994 she obtained a law degree from New York University. Stead worked as a public defender and did some writing on the side.

After her young son accidentally broke her laptop and all her previous adult-oriented writing was lost, Stead decided that it was time to find something new to write about. After rereading the books that she enjoyed as a child, she discovered her passion for writing books for young adults. Her first book, *First Light* (2007), was inspired by an article that Stead read. The book is centered on the adventures of a 12-year-old boy in Greenland. The novel is the meeting point of fantasy, adventure, and scientific findings about climate change. Stead's second novel, *When You Reach Me* (2009), is about a girl named Miranda living in New York City. Miranda's life takes an unexpected turn when she starts receiving mysterious letters warning her of imminent danger. *Liar & Spy* (2012), set in Brooklyn, N.Y., pairs a seventh-grade bullied outcast and a homeschooled loner who team up to spy on a suspicious neighbor.

# AMY TAN

(b. 1952– )

he overwhelming success that Amy Tan achieved with her first novel, *The Joy Luck Club* (1989), resulted in part from

the vividness of her recollections of growing up as a Chinese American. Although
the novel dealt with the problematic relationships between Chinese-born parents
and their Americanized children, Tan was
reluctant to be considered a spokesperson
for Asian Americans. She felt she was dealing with a personal conflict rather than with
the raising of political consciousness. More
important, she wanted her literary accom-
plishments to be regarded as aesthetic
creations rather than as vehicles for cultural
or historical edification, and the success of
her subsequent novels did indeed establish
Tan as a notable literary presence whose
best sellers generated widespread, multi-
ethnic appeal.

Amy Tan was born in Oakland, Calif.
on Feb. 19, 1952, approximately two and a
half years after her parents emigrated from
China. Growing up in the San Francisco
Bay area, she was fiercely opposed to her
Chinese background in her youth, and she
even went as far as sleeping with a clothes-
pin on her nose hoping to narrow its Asian
shape. After Tan's father and her older
brother died from brain tumours within
eight months of each other in 1968, her

*Amy Tan.* Amy Tierney/WireImage/Getty Images

mother revealed that she had three daughters from a previous marriage still living in China. Tan felt sure that she was, in her own words, "the wicked daughter," so she became more rebellious and rejected her background with a renewed vigour.

After this family tragedy, Tan's mother took her and her younger brother to live in Europe. Tan finished high school in Montreux, Switzerland, and the family returned to the United States shortly thereafter. She attended numerous institutions before receiving a master's degree in linguistics from San Jose State University in 1976. After graduation, she worked as a consultant for developmentally disabled children until she turned to freelance writing in the early 1980s.

As a release from working 90 hours a week as a well-established business writer, Tan decided in 1985 to pursue her dream of writing fiction. She attended a writer's workshop, read lots of fiction, and began writing a short story. The short story she composed, called "Endgame," was about a young girl's success as a chess champion. "Endgame" eventually became a part of *The Joy Luck Club*, a novel that actually began as a series of short stories written for magazines.

*The Joy Luck Club* related the experiences of four Chinese mothers, their Chinese American daughters, and the struggle of the two generations to communicate with one another. Tan was strongly motivated to write this novel when, after her mother was hospitalized because of an apparent heart attack, Tan decided to get to know her mother better, take her to China, and write a book. Finally, upon meeting two of her half sisters on her trip to China with her mother in 1987, she felt a sense of belonging, and she reflected this feeling and wove parts of her mother's life into *The Joy Luck Club*. Tan's first novel met with instant critical and commercial success. It became the longest running best seller on the *New York Times* best seller list in 1989, won the Bay Area Book Reviewers Award and the Commonwealth Gold Award, and was nominated for the National Book Award and the National Book Critics Circle Award. The book was also made into a feature film, for which Tan cowrote the screenplay.

Tan followed her first successful novel with a second novel, *The Kitchen God's Wife*, in 1991. As with her first novel, her style was infused with flashbacks, storytelling, and a strong sense of history. Her second novel became a number one best seller on the *New York Times* hardcover list. In *The Hundred Secret Senses* (1995), an American woman gradually learns to appreciate her Chinese half sister and the knowledge she imparts. Tan again explored the complex relationships of mothers and daughters in *The Bonesetter's Daughter* (2001), in which a woman cares for her mother, who is afflicted with Alzheimer disease. In *Saving Fish from Drowning* (2005), a San Francisco art dealer narrates the story of a group of tourists traveling through China and Myanmar (Burma). *The Rules for Virgins* (2011) takes readers back to the Shanghai of 1912 and the world of sexual encounters. Tan also published a collection of essays, *The Opposite of Fate: A Book of Musings* (2003), and the children's stories *The Moon Lady* (1992) and *The Chinese Siamese Cat* (1994; adapted as a television series in 2001).

# JOHN UPDIKE

(b. 1932–d. 2009)

John Updike was one of the most famous and successful writers of his generation.

Updike explored such diverse themes as religion, adultery, and art in his many novels, short stories, poems, essays, and articles. In muscular, poetic prose, Updike painted remarkably vivid portraits of American life and culture.

John Hoyer Updike was born in Reading, Pa. on March 18, 1932. His family lived in the small town of Shillington before moving to a farmhouse when Updike was 13 years old. He won a scholarship to Harvard, where he studied English and graduated summa cum laude in 1954. Updike briefly studied painting at the Ruskin School of Drawing and Fine Art in Oxford, Eng., before returning to the United States to work at the *New Yorker*. There, he wrote for the "Talk of the Town" section and contributed short stories, essays, poetry, and book reviews from 1955 to 1957.

Updike won many awards and honours throughout his lifetime. His first novel, *Poorhouse Fair* (1959), won the Rosenthal Foundation Award of the National Institute of Arts and Letters, and his 1959 Guggenheim Fellowship gave him the freedom to write his second novel, *Rabbit, Run*. Published in 1960, *Rabbit, Run* was the first of a series of novels that tells the story of Harry (Rabbit) Angstrom, a former high school basketball star struggling with the mundane realities of marriage and parent-hood in suburban America. Although *Rabbit Redux* (1971) received a lukewarm reception, *Rabbit Is Rich* (1981) won the National Book Critics Circle Award, the American Book Award, and the Pulitzer Prize. The final Rabbit novel, *Rabbit at Rest* (1990), earned Updike a second Pulitzer Prize in 1991.

Throughout his career, Updike revisited characters from his earlier novels, extending their stories. Updike wrote a trilogy of novels centering on the character Henry Bech: *Bech: A Book* (1970), *Bech Is Back* (1982), and *Bech at Bay* (1998). Likewise, the coven of witches from Updike's 1984 novel, *The Witches of Eastwick,* reappears—30 years older—in the 2008 sequel *The Widows of Eastwick.*

Unafraid to tackle taboo subjects, Updike's 1968 novel *Couples* explores in remarkable detail the sexual life and moral ambiguities of the late 1960s. *Toward the End of Time* (1997) examines issues of religion, faith, and roots in the lives of four generations of a family. The 2006 novel *Terrorist* addresses the cul-tural shifts that occurred in the United States following the September 11 attacks. Updike possessed a finely tuned sense of time and place, and few writers have depicted modern American life with such power, beauty, and understanding.

In addition to his novels, Updike produced several volumes of poetry, collections of short stories, and criticism. His 1983 essay collection, *Hugging the Shore*, won the National Book Critics Circle Award for Criticism. *Due Considerations* (2007) collects his later commentary on topics such as art, sexuality, and literature. Updike published his autobiography, *Self-Consciousness: Memoirs,* in 1989. A rare writer whose works are both popularly and critically acclaimed, Updike wrote constantly and his creative output was prodigious. He died on January 27, 2009, in Danvers, Mass.

# KURT VONNEGUT, JR.

(b. 1922–d. 2007)

Characterized by grim humour and a preoccupation with the hostile forces of science and technology, Kurt Vonnegut, Jr., wrote numerous novels in which he pleads for human kindness in the present world and in the dehumanized world he depicts as the future.

Vonnegut was born on Nov. 11, 1922, in Indianapolis, Ind. He attended Cornell University before serving in the United States Air Force in World War II. As a German prisoner of war, Vonnegut was a survivor of the fire bombing of Dresden, Ger., in February 1945. After the war Vonnegut studied anthropology at the University of Chicago and worked as a police reporter and a public relations writer before leaving to write full-time.

Vonnegut began his writing career with short stories for magazines. His first novel, *Player Piano*, was published in 1952, followed by *The Sirens of Titan* (1959), *Mother Night* (1961), and *God Bless You, Mr. Rosewater* (1965). Vonnegut gained attention from the critics and the reading public with *Cat's Cradle* (1963). His best-known work, *Slaughterhouse-Five, or The Children's Crusade* (1969), is an autobiographical but fictional recreation of the Dresden bombing as experienced by a naive American soldier, Billy Pilgrim, imprisoned in a meat storage cellar below a slaughterhouse.

Later novels include *Breakfast of Champions* (1973), *Slapstick* (1976), *Jailbird* (1979), *Deadeye Dick* (1982), *Galápagos* (1985), *Bluebeard* (1987), *Hocus Pocus* (1990), and *Timequake* (1997). Vonnegut also wrote the play *Happy Birthday, Wanda June* (1970), the collection of short stories *Welcome to the Monkey House* (1968), and the nonfiction works *Wampeters, Foma & Grandfalloons* (1974), *Palm Sunday* (1981), and *A Man Without a Country* (2005). Vonnegut died on April 11, 2007, in New York, N.Y. Works published after his death include *Armageddon in Retrospect* (2008), a collection of fiction and nonfiction that focuses on war and peace, and a number of previously unpublished short stories, assembled in *Look at the Birdie* (2009) and *While Mortals Sleep* (2011). *We Are What We Pretend to Be* (2012) comprised an early unpublished novella and a fragment of a novel unfinished at his death. A selection of his correspondence was published as *Letters* (2012).

# ALICE WALKER

(b. 1944– )

Alice Walker is an American writer whose novels, short stories, and poems

are noted for their insightful treatment of African American culture. Her novels, most notably *The Color Purple* (1982), focus particularly on women.

Born Feb. 9, 1944, in Eatonton, Ga., Walker was the eighth child of African American sharecroppers. While growing up she was accidentally blinded in one eye, and her mother gave her a typewriter, allowing her to write instead of doing chores. She received a scholarship to attend Spelman College, where she studied for two years before transferring to Sarah Lawrence College. After graduating in 1965, Walker moved to Mississippi and became involved in the civil rights movement. She also began teaching and publishing short stories and essays. She married Melryn Lerenthal in 1967, but the couple divorced in 1976.

Walker's first book of poetry, *Once*, appeared in 1968, and her first novel, *The Third Life of Grange Copeland* (1970), a narrative that spans 60 years and three generations, followed two years later. A second volume of poetry, *Revolutionary Petunias and Other Poems*, and her first collection of short stories, *In Love and Trouble: Stories of Black Women*, both appeared in 1973. After moving to New

York, Walker completed *Meridian* (1976), a novel describing the coming of age of several civil rights workers in the 1960s.

Walker later moved to California, where she wrote her most popular novel, *The Color Purple* (1982), which depicts the growing up and self-realization of an African American woman between 1909 and 1947 in a town in Georgia. The book won a Pulitzer Prize and was adapted into a film by Steven Spielberg in 1985. A musical version produced by Oprah Winfrey and Quincy Jones premiered in 2004.

Walker's later fiction includes *The Temple of My Familiar* (1989), *Possessing the Secret of Joy* (1992), *By the Light of My Father's Smile* (1998), and *Now Is the Time to Open Your Heart* (2005). Reviewers complained that these novels employed New Age abstractions and poorly conceived characters, though Walker continued to draw praise for championing racial and gender equality in her work. She also released the volume of short stories *The Way Forward Is with a Broken Heart* (2000) and several other volumes of poetry, including *Absolute Trust in the Goodness of the Earth* (2003) and *A Poem Traveled Down My Arm* (2003). *Her Blue Body Everything*

*We Know: Earthling Poems* (1991) collects poetry from 1965 to 1990.

Her essays were compiled in *In Search of Our Mother's Gardens: Womanist Prose* (1983), *Sent by Earth: A Message from the Grandmother Spirit After the Bombing of the World Trade Center and Pentagon* (2001), *We Are the Ones We Have Been Waiting For* (2006), and *The Cushion in the Road: Meditation and Wandering as the Whole World Awakens to Being in Harm's Way* (2013). Walker also wrote juvenile fiction and critical essays on such female writers as Flannery O'Connor and Zora Neale Hurston. She cofounded a short-lived press in 1984.

# DAVID FOSTER WALLACE

(b. 1962–d. 2008)

U.S. novelist, short-story writer, and essayist David Foster Wallace wrote dark, often satirical analyses of American culture. He is perhaps best known for his second novel, *Infinite Jest* (1996), which is a complex story blending topics such as addiction, consumerism, tennis, depression, and family relationships—all seen in a future world. *Infinite Jest* was notably the first of Wallace's works to feature what was to become his stylistic hallmark: the prominent use of notes (in this case, endnotes), which were his attempt to reproduce the nonlinearity of human thought on the page.

Wallace was born on Feb. 21, 1962, in Ithaca, N.Y., to a philosophy professor and an English teacher. He received a bachelor's degree from Amherst College in 1985. As he was completing a master's degree in creative writing at the University of Arizona, his highly regarded debut novel, *The Broom of the System* (1987), was published. He later taught creative writing at Illinois State University and at Pomona College. He received a MacArthur Foundation fellowship grant in 1997.

*Infinite Jest* is a massive, multilayered novel that took Wallace four years to write. A sweeping cast of postmodern characters appear, ranging from recovering alcoholics and foreign statesmen to residents of a halfway house and high-school tennis stars. In the novel advertising has become widespread, and the populace is addicted to consumerism. Even the calendar years have been named by companies that purchased the rights to promote their products. Wallace's meandering writing style variously exhilarated and maddened critics, who often compared *Infinite Jest* to the novels of Thomas Pynchon and Don DeLillo.

Wallace's collections of short stories include *Girl with Curious Hair* (1989), *Brief Interviews with Hideous Men* (1999), and *Oblivion* (2004). His essays, often on such simple subjects as the Illinois State Fair, talk radio, and luxury cruises—yet still full of footnotes—are collected in *A Supposedly Fun Thing I'll Never Do Again* (1997) and *Consider the Lobster, and Other Essays* (2005). *Everything and More: A Compact History of Infinity* (2003) is a survey of the mathematical concept of infinity. He also wrote, with Mark Costello, *Signifying Rappers: Rap and Race in the Urban Present* (1997).

Wallace had suffered from depression since his early 20s, and, after numerous failed attempts to find an effective drug therapy, he took his own life on Sept. 12, 2008, in Claremont, Calif. Another novel, *The Pale King* (2011), was published after his death. The book, which Wallace left unfinished,

*David Foster Wallace.* Steve Liss/Time & Life Pictures/Getty *Images*

was assembled by Michael Pietsch, Wallace's longtime editor. Its central theme centers on boredom as a potential means of attaining bliss—an alternative to the culture of overstimulation that was the main subject of *Infinite Jest*. A third collection of his nonfiction writing, *Both Flesh and Not* (2012), was also published posthumously.

# PAUL ZINDEL

(b. 1936–d. 2003)

U.S. playwright and author Paul Zindel was born on May 15, 1936, on Staten Island, N.Y. His plays and novels combined elements of fantasy, science fiction, and humour to create a highly individualized style.

Zindel attended Wagner College, from which he received a bachelor's degree in 1958 and a master's degree the following year. He taught high school chemistry for ten years before turning to writing plays and children's books. His play *The Effect of Gamma Rays on Man-in-the-Moon Marigolds* (1964) won several awards, including an Obie Award and a Pulitzer Prize for Drama. It told the story of two sisters and their overbearing mother. Parents and adolescents alike found the play appealing and unerring in its view of young adulthood. Zindel's novels included *The Pigman* (1968), *My Darling, My Hamburger* (1969), *Pardon Me, You're Stepping on my Eyeball* (1974), *I Love My Mother* (1975), *The Undertaker's Gone Bananas!* (1979), *The Girl Who Wanted a Boy* (1982),

*Harry and Hortense at Hormone High* (1984), *A Begonia for Miss Applebaum* (1989), and *David & Della* (1993). Zindel broke new ground in 1994 with the horror story *Loch*, which he followed with *The Doom Stone* (1995) and *Reef of Death* (1998). These all were written for an audience of young adults.

Zindel was criticized for a moralizing tone that was evident in several of his books, but he received praise for accurately reproducing the nuances of youthful dialogue. Zindel's other plays included *And Miss Reardon Drinks a Little* (1971), *Let Me Hear You Whisper: A Play* (1974), and *Ladies at the Alamo* (1975). Several of his works were adapted for television and motion pictures. Zindel died in New York City on March 27, 2003.

# MARKUS ZUSAK

(b. 1975– )

M arkus Zusak is an Australian author best known for writing young adult novels that focus on the themes of hardship and determination. His works include *I Am the Messenger* (2005, originally published in Australia as *The Messenger* in 2002) and *The Book Thief* (2006).

Zusak was born June 23, 1975 in Sydney, Australia. Zusak is the youngest of four children. His parents, a housepainter and a maid, did not read or write English when they immigrated to Australia from Germany and Austria. Zusak began writing fiction when he was 16 years old. He studied at the University of Sydney and worked as a janitor and a high school English teacher before turning to fiction writing full-time.

Zusak began his career as a novelist with a series of novels about two brothers, Cameron and Ruben Wolfe, from an disadvantaged Australian family trying to make their way in life: *The Underdogs* (1999), *Fighting Ruben Wolfe* (2000), and *When Dogs Cry* (2001, published in the United States as *Getting the Girl* in 2003). *Fighting Ruben Wolfe* tells the story of the boys' attempts to make money fighting in illegal boxing matches. Although Cameron, "the Underdog," struggles, his brother easily adapts to fighting in the ring and earns the nickname "Fighting Ruben Wolfe." The novel climaxes when Cameron and Ruben have to face each other in the ring. Zusak's fourth novel, *I Am the Messenger*, tells the story of Ed Kennedy, a 19-year-old taxi driver whose directionless life takes on new meaning when, after preventing a bank robbery, he begins finding mysterious messages written on playing cards in his mailbox. The messages send him to various places where people need help. *The Book Thief* was published as an adult novel in Australia and as a young adult novel in the United States. Narrated by Death, *The Book Thief* tells the story of Liesel Meminger, an orphaned girl who comes of age in Germany during World War II. The novel was a *New York Times* best seller for many years, as well as a Printz Honor book.

# Glossary

**accolade** A mark of recognition of merit; praise.

**adultery** Voluntary sexual intercourse between a married person and someone other than his or her spouse.

**allegory** A story in which the characters and events are symbols that stand for truths about human life.

**apocalypse** An event in which destruction or damage occurs on a catastrophic scale.

**asylum** Protection given, especially to political refugees.

**attrition** A reduction in numbers usually as a result of resignation, retirement, or death.

**burka** A loose garment that covers the head, face, and body and is worn in public by certain Muslim women.

**coven** A meeting or band of witches.

**cum laude** With distinction; with honors. (Summa cum laude means with the highest distinction.)

**dualism** The quality or state of having a dual nature.

**dystopian** Describing an imaginary place where people lead dehumanized and often fearful lives.

**envoy** A diplomatic representative.

**exuberant** Joyfully enthusiastic.

**golem** In Jewish folklore, a golem is an artificial figure made to represent a human being endowed with life.

**Igbo** A member of a people of the area around the lower Niger in Africa.

**induct** To admit as a member.

**kibbutz** A farming settlement in Israel that is owned and shared equally by the people who live there and run it. (Kibbutzim is the plural form of kibbutz.)

**libretto** The text of an opera or musical.

**melodramatic** Marked by exaggerated emotions.

**mundane** Having to do with the ordinary, practical details of everyday life.

**ordination** The act of being ordained, that is, to make a person a Christian minister or priest by a special ceremony.

**picaresque** Of, relating to, or being a type of fiction that presents the adventures of a usually rascally character.

**pluralistic** A state of society in which members of diverse ethnic, racial, religious, or social groups maintain an autonomous participation in and development of their traditional culture or special interest within the confines of a common civilization.

**posthumous** Published after the death of the author.

**prolific** Highly productive.

**protagonist** The chief character in a play, novel, or story.

**ribald** Marked by or using coarse or indecent language or humor.

**rogue** A mischievous individual.

**taboo** Something banned on grounds of morality or taste.

**totalitarian** Of or relating to a political system in which the government has complete control over the people.

**trickster** One who tricks, such as a dishonest person who cheats others by trickery.

**Waffen-SS** The armed SS, the SS being a unit of Nazis created as bodyguard to Adolf Hitler and later expanded to take charge of intelligence, central security, policing action, and the mass extermination of those they considered inferior or undesirable.

**womanist** A term coined by U.S. writer and feminist Alice Walker to specify a black feminist.

# For More Information

Center for Fiction
17 East 47th Street
New York, NY 10017
(212) 755-6710
Web site: http://www.centerforfiction.org
The Center for Fiction is a nonprofit literary organization devoted to celebrating popular fiction through public events, including panels, lectures, and conversations with authors hosted at its New York headquarters. It also recognizes important works of fiction through its annual awards and provides resources for emerging writers and readers of fiction alike.

John Updike Society
Department of English
Illinois Wesleyan University
Bloomington, IL 61702
(309) 556-3352
Web site: http://blogs.iwu.edu/johnupdikesociety
The John Updike Society was founded in 2009 for the sake of awakening and maintaining interest among readers in the writings and life of John Updike. To facilitate study and discussion of the author's works, the society holds conferences, publishes the annual critical journal the *John Updike Review,* and

is building an archive for researchers and other educational activities at Alvernia University.

Kurt Vonnegut Memorial Library
The Emelie Building
340 North Senate Avenue
Indianapolis, IN 46204
(317) 652-1954
Web site: http://www.vonnegutlibrary.org
The Kurt Vonnegut Memorial Library operates both to deepen the study of Kurt Vonnegut's works through its collection of his personal items, artwork, and manuscripts and to promote the popular fiction literary scene from its Indianapolis building. It hosts lectures, readings, and other events for both local and visiting authors, and showcases popular fiction and other literary works in its annual publication *So It Goes: The Literary Journal of the Kurt Vonnegut Memorial Library*.

National Book Foundation
90 Broad Street, Suite 604
New York, NY 10004
(212) 685-0261
Web site: http://www.nationalbook.org

Since 1950, the National Book Foundation
has been the organization behind the
National Book Awards (NBA), dedicated to recognizing and promoting
the best in literary production in the
United States. In addition to its NBA
activities, the foundation also works to
promote literacy and discussion of contemporary writing on high school and
college school campuses and through
reading clubs in cities across America.

PEN Canada
24 Ryerson Avenue, Suite 301
Toronto, ON M5T 2P3
Canada
(416) 703-8448
Web site: http://pencanada.ca
PEN Canada is dedicated to promoting
and encouraging literature and the
freedom of expression of the literary
community in Canada. To that end, the
organization promotes the readership
of popular writers, both international
and Canadian, and discussion of their
works and the contributions they have
made to society at large. Its "Ideas in
Dialogue" literary series hosts conversations with famous writers.

Penticton Writers and Publishers (PWAP)
4011 Finnerty Road
Penticton, BC V2A 8W2
Canada
(250) 492-0629
Web site: http://www.penwriters.com
The PWAP is a group started in 1994
   dedicated to promoting the writing and
   publishing industries in British Columbia.
   In addition to publishing anthologies of
   literature and hosting monthly writers
   groups, it plans events for teen readers
   in the area, including the Raise a Reader
   youth literacy program, which hosts author
   visits to area schools and the annual British
   Columbia Youth Writers Camp for teens
   across the province.

## Web Sites

Due to the changing nature of Internet
links, Rosen Educational Services has developed an online list of Web sites related
to the subject of this book. This site is
updated regularly. Please use this link to
access the list:

http://www.rosenlinks.com/eafct/fict

# For Further Reading

Abrams, Dennis, and Elisa Ludwig. *Judy Blume*. New York, NY: Chelsea House, 2009.

Axelrod-Contrada, Joan. *Isabel Allende*. New York, NY: Benchmark, 2010.

Bloom, Harold. *Khaled Hosseini's The Kite Runner* (Bloom's Guides). New York, NY: Chelsea House, 2009.

Bloom, Harold. *Cormac McCarthy*. New York, NY: Chelsea House, 2009.

Hagler, Gina. *Sarah Dessen*. New York, NY: Rosen Publishing, 2014.

Lew, Kristi. *Laurie Halse Anderson*. New York, NY: Rosen Publishing, 2014.

Lusted, Marcia Amidon. *Suzanne Collins: Words on Fire*. Minneapolis, MN: 21st Century, 2012.

Nelson, David. *Women's Issues in Margaret Atwood's The Handmaid's Tale*. San Diego, CA: Greenhaven, 2011.

Sonneborn, Liz. *Sherman Alexie*. New York, NY: Rosen Publishing, 2012.

Welsch, Camille-Yvette. *Meg Cabot*. New York, NY: Chelsea House, 2008.

# Index